Climbing Your Career Tree

Life Lessons to Grow the Leader Within You

David Purvis

Printed in the United States of America

First printing, 2026

ISBN: SBN 979-8-9910089-4-5

Published by: 1 Stage Media

Your Free Bonus Resources

Thank you for reading *Climbing Your Career Tree*. As a reader, you have exclusive access to free leadership tools designed to help you put these principles into action immediately.

These practical resources will help you assess where you are, identify your biggest challenges, and build a clear plan to move forward with confidence.

Visit www.davidpurvis.com/book-resources to download for free.

Table of Contents

Dedication

To Susanne: my wife, partner, and confidante over all these years.

With your love and support, I have grown in ways that I didn't think were possible.

Introduction

What if I told you that you have been thinking about your career progression all wrong? Whether you are just entering the workforce, moving into leadership roles, or reaching the final stages of your career, you are probably thinking about what you need to do to climb the corporate career ladder. But you have the wrong model.

Over almost four decades in the oil and gas industry, I climbed that "corporate ladder," moving from individual contributor roles up through multiple levels of leadership, ultimately serving in senior executive roles at two international corporations. I now own the majority share of a partnership focused on coaching business owners and nonprofits in the Greater New Orleans area.

As I neared the end of my corporate roles, I realized that the concept of a career ladder was not the best description of career progression. I had really been growing and climbing my Career Tree.

Consider some of the following scenarios you might face in your career:

- Imagine that you are halfway through your university degree, but don't like the job opportunities available to you. What are you supposed to do?

- Or, you have just been promoted to a supervisor role after years as an individual contributor. What does it take to be successful? Where is that handbook to help you figure out how to be successful in your new role?

- What if, as a new manager, several of your peers are now your direct reports? How do you transition from colleague to leader without sacrificing your working relationships?

- Or, as you lead a significant project, you find yourself misaligned with senior leaders on the right course of action. This disconnect could threaten your job. How should you proceed?

As part of my journey through various roles and leadership levels, I faced each of the problems above and several more. From these experiences, I learned numerous lessons in leadership. Some were easy to learn, some were hard, and some had to be repeated multiple times before they truly sank into my thick skull. Whether easy or hard, each lesson was valuable in shaping me as an engaging, caring, and effective leader.

Over the years, I had several effective leaders and mentors who helped me learn some of the lessons noted in the book. But I had to learn several on my own. As I move into semi-retirement, I am entering the phase of my life where I enjoy giving back and helping others.

I hope that as you read through some of the experiences from my journey, you will discover tips for successfully growing and climbing your own Career Tree. I also hope that you will find that many of the Life Lessons given can be applied to help you grow into the best leader you can be.

Chapter 1

Growing and Climbing Your Career Tree

During my last corporate role as VP Engineering for the BHP – Petroleum organization, one of my areas of accountability was the professional development, deployment, and advancement of the 300+ engineering staff. One important focus area was the recruitment and early-career development of junior staff. To build a better relationship with this work group, I held regular breakfast meetings to discuss questions they may have regarding company policies, training, career progression, and sometimes just life in general.

One of the most common questions from the engineers with 2 to 5 years of experience was when they could become a supervisor and lead a group. In these conversations, they expressed confidence in their skills and capabilities to be a successful supervisor and were eager to move up the career ladder. While I was not their direct supervisor, I was seen as the top "engineer" in the Petroleum division since the word engineer was in my title and I sat on the Executive Leadership Team. On the organization chart, my role was often three levels above them. Some of the more direct and driven junior staff often asked exactly what roles they needed to take in order to climb the ladder to get to a role like mine (and how long it would take).

In these discussions, I had concerns about discussing career progression just in terms of a career ladder. I shared my thoughts that using a ladder analogy for your career implied that the only way to move was *up* or *down*. After multiple discussions, I introduced the idea of a **Career Tree**.

First, what is a career? A common definition from the Merriam-Webster dictionary is 1) a profession for which one trains, and which is undertaken as a permanent calling; and 2) a pursuit of consecutive progressive achievement, especially in public, professional, or business life. As we think of a person's career, most people will stay in the workforce for 30 to 40 years. With this background, I propose that we think of a career in three segments: Early, Mid, and Late Career.

These segments aren't necessarily equal in duration, but each comes with its own objectives for success. Let's look at each, how it fits into the whole of your career, and why a Career Tree is a better descriptor for your career journey. I will share some of my personal experiences and leadership lessons from each career segment.

EARLY CAREER – PLANT THE SEED, GROW DEEP ROOTS, AND BUILD A STRONG TRUNK

Using the stages of tree growth as an analogy for success as an employee or entrepreneur, the early years of your career are the time to find or improve the soil at the location you choose to plant your tree, to grow deep roots, and build a strong trunk. Key focus areas for this segment of your career should be:

- Choosing the area of work that fits your interests and skills
- Building your core skills
- Accelerating foundational skills on the path to functional excellence
- Becoming known for being good at your craft
- Beginning to build your professional network (not just your group of close friends). Your network should include people from within your company, within your industry, and within your community, and should include:
  - Peers – roughly the same point in your careers, both in your core skill area and in other disciplines.
  - Colleagues and teammates – those you work closely with on a daily basis.
- Obtain or accept a mentor – generally someone more senior than yourself. Your mentor(s) provide guidance on navigating the path forward in a specific area. You should seek out mentors:
  - In your technical/operational arena
  - Who understand the business/financial side of your industry
  - Internally in the area of office dynamics (a PC way of saying office politics)

Your high school, university, and the first few years of your career are when you **plant the seeds** of your career and start to grow solid roots. Progressing into part-time jobs, furthering your education or trade, or taking on internships or apprenticeships is comparable to watching a seed grow into a sapling. During this time, you will start to learn the type of work you like to do (and more importantly, what you don't like). Getting work experience will help confirm that you have chosen a career path that works for you. Based on the pace of building your skills and developing your network, the **Early Career** phase of your overall career will cover your **first 5 to 10 years** of work.

After a few years of work, you may find that you have planted the seed for your **Career Tree** in the wrong place (wrong focus, wrong company, or wrong industry). This doesn't mean that all is lost. We can use our analogy to *reseed* your **Career Tree,** focusing on changing what didn't work before. A key to personal and professional happiness is ensuring, as soon as possible, that your Career Tree is planted in the right place. You don't want to have to reseed when your tree is fully grown and in bloom.

MID-CAREER – BRANCHING OUT

In the tree analogy, after planting your roots and growing your trunk during your early career, your mid-career period is when you have the opportunity to **branch out** beyond your core skill area. From a timing standpoint, this career period generally spans from 7 years to 15+ years of experience. In many companies, the cadre of mid-career staff can be considered the engine of the organization. They generate a large quantity of high-quality work product. As an individual, during this period, you should be growing the branches of your Career Tree. Key activities can and may include:

- Undertake broadening assignments outside of your core discipline to grow your skill set and gain a larger perspective of your industry

- Expand your professional network
- Start first-level supervisory and mid-level management roles

Broadening assignments – Depending on the opportunities within your company, this is a time to broaden your skill set. You may have a chance to take a special assignment in another discipline. This type of assignment may present some struggles as you move out of the comfort zone of your core skill set. In the long run, taking such a move can enhance your overall capability and potential. Think of it as adding branches to the trunk of your tree that, when fully grown, will provide a broader canopy. A key to success when taking a broadening assignment is to put your full effort into growing your new skill set. No resting on your laurels.

Expand networks – having established your credentials and capabilities during your early career phase, the mid-career period is the time to expand your network. With strong foundational skills, you are now ready to be a mentor and/or advisor to more junior staff. You can also start engaging in industry events. If you aren't directly asked to be a mentor or participate in industry activities, don't be afraid to ask. Show initiative by putting yourself forward. This is also a period to build stronger relationships with senior staff and leaders, as that is the next phase in your career tree. This expanded network adds further branches to your career tree.

Supervision/management roles – if you choose a career path of supervision/management, you will often take your first supervisor role in the 6-to-10-year range. As I discussed with the early-career staff in my VP role, experience has shown that when an individual starts a supervisory role earlier than this, they often lack the core skill foundation and interpersonal maturity to guide and review the work of others, some of whom may be older and more experienced. I will give some examples of learnings and positive traits of good supervisors in later chapters.

LATE CAREER – GROWING IN STATURE AND BEARING FRUIT

Your late career period extends from roughly 15 to 20 years of experience to the end of your working life. As you enter this phase, you have already chosen a primary path: either an individual contributor or a management path. During this stage, irrespective of the path you've chosen, you will grow your stature and bear fruit, helping others grow and succeed as well. By choosing to stay as an individual contributor as you progress through your mid-career period, you will likely have specialized in a specific area of focus. As you enter the late-career phase, you start to be known as a Subject Matter Expert and will be called upon for advice and mentoring. As a senior leader, you will be taking on greater responsibility for leading teams, groups of teams, and even large organizations. The higher you climb in your Career Tree, the more your time horizon shifts from day/month/year to visioning for the future. Note: even if you choose the management branch, there may be times when you will undertake an individual contributor role to help further broaden your skills and perspectives to prepare you for even larger roles.

I will share more on the challenges in transitioning from one role to the next in a later chapter.

CAREER TREE OVERVIEW

Early Career – first 5 to 10 years – Plant the seed, grow deep roots, and build your trunk

- Build your core skills
- Accelerate foundational skills on the path to functional excellence
- Start your professional network
- Obtain or accept a mentor

Mid-Career – 7 to 15+ years of experience – Branching out

- Consider broadening assignments to increase your perspective
- Expand your network, including those outside your industry
- Supervisor/management roles (if you choose this branch)

Late Career – 15+ years to the end of your working years – Growing in Stature and Bearing Fruit

- Leveraging your experience and expertise
- Advise and mentor junior staff
- Expand horizons to impact the path and success of the organization

CAREER TREE

Individual Contributor

Management

Senior Advisor

Senior Leader

Late Career
15+ years of experience

Specialize
Build Depth/
Breadth

Business Judgment
Strategy
Execution

Work Engine
Special Assignments
Role Choices

Mid-Career
7 – 15+ years of experience

First Supervisor Role
+/- 7 years of experience

Build Core Skills
Functional Excellence
Find a Mentor

Early Career
0 – 10 years of experience

Early Career

Planting the Seed, Growing Deep Roots,
and Building Your Trunk

Chapter 2

Planting the Seed – Knowing Yourself and Getting Out of Your Comfort Zone

A critical part of any career is starting out in the right spot. Determining where to plant your seed, how to feed and water to build deep and solid roots, and starting to grow a big, beautiful Career Tree is not easy. In this chapter, I will share some stories from my own early steps during high school and university, from learning to push myself, to value the differences of others, to figuring out what I did and didn't like to do, and pushing through tragedy. I will also share some of the Life Lessons I learned that will hopefully give you some guidance on these first steps to success.

WHAT DO YOU DO WHEN YOU DON'T FIT THE DEFINITION OF NORMAL?

A bit of background first. I grew up in rural Mississippi and was a teenager in the mid to late 1970s. In those days, the definition of normal for teenage boys in that part of the US was to be active in sports, enjoy hunting and fishing, and do okay at school.

Well, that wasn't me. I was never very big. My senior year of high school, I was maybe 5' 3" and at most weighed 110 pounds. A starting position on any of the HS sports teams was never going to happen. And instead of hunting and fishing, I enjoyed reading books and excelling in my classes at school, especially math and science. I was on a path to be the valedictorian. Needless to say, I stood out but not in the "normal" way. I was the "nerd" of the senior class, which came with its expected level of teasing.

EARLY LIFE LESSON – PUSH YOURSELF TO BE BETTER

During my senior year of high school, four of us rising seniors petitioned our county school board to allow us to take advanced math. We were all interested in focusing on STEM university degrees. For our high school, advanced math meant Trigonometry and Algebra 3/Pre-Calculus. Our teacher had several decades of teaching math but was new to our school, so she didn't have any history with any of us from prior classes. When the four of us would come to class to take a test, she would tell us to "grab a corner." She said it wasn't that she didn't trust us, but why make temptation easy?

As the semester progressed, I was talking with the teacher one day after class. She stated that I should be doing more in her class. If she assigned the class 10 problems for homework, she thought I should be doing 20. As any "normal" teenager would, in my brash manner (and not really respecting my elders), I asked WHY since I had the top grade in the class and was easily on my way to getting an A. But she saw something in me that I didn't see in myself. She thought I could excel, while I thought I was already good enough. As you might expect, I didn't take her advice. I was a nerd, but I wasn't that big of a nerd.

It all came home to roost in the final week of HS. According to school policy, I was exempt from the Advanced Math final. However, the teacher told me that no one was exempt from her exams, and I had to take the final to graduate. And what a final it was. Since I had "assumed" I was exempt, I had accepted a time slot to work my job at the local grocery store and missed the scheduled final. When I arrived at school the next day, the teacher informed me that I must take a make-up final. As it was the last week of school, the exam would be the next day. When I showed up to her classroom during my study hall period to take my make-up final, I had my own special version with two "proofs." She said it was a different exam, as she didn't know if I had spoken to the other three classmates about the test. (I also think it was a bit harder as a way of emphasizing that I should have paid attention to her advice earlier in the semester and dug deeper into the concepts, versus just doing the minimum. But I will never know.) After eating humble pie, I asked for a hint to get started and ultimately finished the test. It was not my best showing, but it was a good learning experience.

LEARNING POINT – Don't be complacent. Just because you are GOOD doesn't mean you can't get BETTER. Never stop learning and growing your skills.

After HS graduation, I decided to go to Mississippi State University to study Chemical Engineering. With two older siblings in nursing school and university, I was going to have to pay for most of my degree through scholarships, work, and loans. It was time to prove that I could make it on my own.

That summer after graduation, my first job was at the County School Bus Barn, courtesy of my father's connections. I was supposed to help change all the tires on the entire fleet of school buses. I think the job was my dad's way of trying to "bulk" me up before heading off to college. Two of my work colleagues were older men who had never graduated from high school, so I had more "book learning" than they did. While maybe not the smartest in book learning, they were very dedicated and hardworking. After watching me break a sweat and break my back for the first few days, they gave me some tips to make the job easier and more efficient. Over the summer, they also taught me to live by faith, enjoy each day, work hard, and do my best at whatever task I had been given.

LEARNING POINT – You can always learn something from everyone you encounter. You just have to be willing to accept the lesson.

NEW HORIZONS AND NEW LESSONS

At the end of the summer, I packed my things and, with the help of my parents, made my way to lovely Starkville, Mississippi, the home of Mississippi State University. Who knew that the previous summer would be one of the last times I would live under my parents' roof for any extended period of time? I was ready to spread my wings and grow – physically and mentally – and expand my circle of friends. It was time to see if the lessons from home had made it through my thick and stubborn head. Adulthood, here I come.

Let's just say it was a stark awakening. My "home" shrunk to a shared 10' x 20' dorm room, communal showers, common kitchen, and den (with the one and only TV). Agreeing on what show to watch was an early lesson in diplomacy and negotiations. (And for you readers under 50, it would be another 20 years before flip-phones were introduced and almost 30 years before streaming services arrived.)

I had two realistic choices: become even more introverted and reserved, or step away from my comfort zone and start engaging with others. After some reflection, prayer, and encouragement from the RA (Resident Advisor) for my wing, I chose to get involved in activities across campus. My decision was also validated by watching my "potluck" (randomly assigned) roommate shrink his world to our dorm room and never get involved.

LEARNING POINT – You can't grow by staying in your comfort zone. Without pushing your limits, you become self-limiting.

One of the first things I did was to join the intramural flag football team for our floor. I even had a starting position as a "rusher." I wasn't the biggest person on the team, but I was pretty quick and agile. I put up a fair number of sacks, which surprised our opponents (and even some of my teammates). We made it to the Intramural playoffs, ultimately losing in the semifinals to one of the Greek teams. It was the best showing by a freshman dorm team in several years, and it was a ton of fun.

While getting involved in dorm activities, intramural sports, and a local church, the first semester of classes was not without its challenges. In fact, the challenges started on the first day of the semester. My first class, Chemistry I, went long. I ran out of the building and hustled over to English I, not my favorite subject. Luckily, I had been sitting in the back row for Chemistry. One of my Chemistry classmates was headed to the same room, and we both arrived shortly after class started. As we walked into the room, the instructor asked us our names. When I said mine, she asked me to meet her after class. In my mind, I thought, "Oh no, it's only my second class period, and I am already in trouble." After the period was over, she asked where I had gone to high school and if I had an older sister. I told her. She told me that she had gone to the same high school and had graduated with my sister. Hallelujah, maybe it was going to be okay. I called my sister that night and asked about the instructor. And just like that, my happy bubble burst. I found out that the two had been rivals in high school. UH OH.

My concern was compounded when I got my first writing assignment back. All I could see was a sea of red. I looked at the top of the paper and saw that my grade was a D+. I had never gotten lower than a B+ before, and only two of those. My vision of excelling at MSU was quickly crashing around my shoulders. However, our instructor said not to worry. The highest grade had been a C+, and our final grade would be based on our progress in writing style and technique, with the last two papers determining our final grade. Taking that guidance to heart, I focused on her feedback and tips on each paper and saw my style and grade steadily improve over each subsequent paper. Either that or she was running out of red ink. With my final two papers, I had earned my A.

Having survived my first semester with a 4.0 GPA, I was ready to tackle the second semester. I was becoming more involved in dorm activities and had even become the assistant to the RA on another floor. It meant moving rooms, but it also meant I got a private room (double the space and no one snoring in my ear at night). On the advice of some upperclassmen in the Chemical Engineering department, I also joined the student chapter of the AIChE organization. (The American Institute of Chemical Engineers is a global professional organization for chemical engineers.)

I didn't realize it at the time, but I was starting to grow my professional network. At the same time, I was also building stronger connections with some of the other residents in the dorm, a few of whom would become lifelong friends. I was broadening my horizons and learning to accept others with different backgrounds (financial, family, faith). I also realized that I needed to lean into the traits and behaviors that had helped me succeed in high school. This meant attending classes, studying hard, treating others with respect, and relying on my faith, including joining a local church and singing in the choir.

I also continued to push myself academically. In the first semester, I had taken Honors Calculus I, even though my highest math in HS was Algebra III/Pre-Calculus. It was a big leap, but I had a great professor and earned my A. Based on that, I signed up for Honors Calculus II with the same professor. As a class, we were all doing well until the 3rd exam when the professor decided to test the limits of our knowledge. Let's just say that I came out of the exam knowing that I had been resting on my laurels and had not done well. I was disappointed but also pleasantly surprised when I got my test back with a score of 79. I found out that it was the 2nd-highest grade out of the class of 16. Not bad, but not great. The frustration came from knowing that the top grade had scored in the 90s and was from a student who was a Pre-Law major and not an Engineering or Math major.

At the end of the semester, the professor told me that I had made a B in the class. I had missed an A by 2 points out of a total of 500. I appealed and asked if he could round my average up to 91, which would be an A, since it was only 2 points off. He told me no, that the top student had a 98 average, and there was too great a difference between the two grades to call them both an A. In his words, "There was an A student, and there were B students." That was tough to hear and brought flashbacks from my HS math teacher. Maybe that lesson hadn't sunk in as deeply as it should have.

REPEAT LEARNING POINT – Don't be complacent. Just because you are GOOD doesn't mean you can't get BETTER. Never stop learning and growing your skills.

I took that setback to heart and focused on my studies for the rest of my undergraduate degree, with the B in Honors Calculus II being the only one I earned at MSU. I was proud of my results that first year and would continue to focus on my academic studies in the remaining years at Mississippi State University. That said, in hindsight, I would say I may have become too focused on my grades at the detriment of expanding my network of contacts, building deeper friendships, and participating in a few more campus sports activities.

LEARNING POINT – Don't become overly focused on one element. Strive for balance in school, work, family, friends, and faith.

I did move back home for three months during the summer after my freshman year. My dad had secured a job for me to work on the line crew with the local power company. As we drove away the first morning with me sitting in the middle of the bench seat between the senior lineman and the junior lineman, I asked what my title was. I'm sure they were thinking, "Who is this little college pipsqueak?" The junior lineman answered me with "You're a grunt." I asked what that meant. He said, "If there is a job I have to do on the job site where I would have to grunt, then that's your job to do." When I got my first paycheck, I learned my real title was *helper*, but I never forgot that I was really a *grunt* and tried to meet the job requirements laid out by the junior lineman.

Our main job that summer was laying a cross-country 3-pole power line. It involved two crews, and the other crew had a college helper as well. As the helpers, our real job was to dig the trenches for the grounding cables between the three poles, by hand, using a spade. In the summer, with no shade. After a couple of weeks, I was longing for my previous summer job changing tires on the bus fleet. At least that had been indoors in the shade. At the end of the summer, my dad asked if I was ready to return to university and resume my studies. My answer was *absolutely*. I had never been so eager to study the next level of Honors Calculus, Organic Chemistry, and Physics. But I did learn an appreciation for those skilled tradesmen who work hard every day to make life easier for others.

LEARNING POINT – It doesn't matter if your job is as a professional, tradesman, or in the service sector. Hard work creates value for others.

After my sophomore year, thanks to one of my scholarships, I had the opportunity to intern at Eastman Chemical Company in Longview, TX. This was my first real experience of being truly on my own. I rented a room from one of the engineers at the plant. I was eager to start work and show that this small-town boy from rural MS could be a contributing member of society. Just lofty thoughts for a 19-year-old.

After arriving at work, I learned that I would be working in an optimization group. My tasks were primarily focused on "rating" heat exchangers throughout the plant, determining their efficiency, and recommending any for cleaning to improve performance. The work was really interesting because it aligned with what I had been learning in my classes at MSU. At the end of the summer, I received very positive feedback from my leaders and was offered the opportunity to return the following summer. However, I never felt comfortable in the plant environment. I wondered if I had chosen the wrong degree.

LEARNING POINT – Knowing what you don't want/like to do is as important as knowing what you love to do.

VALUING THE DIFFERENCES IN OTHERS

Back on campus, I continued with studies in Chemical Engineering, even as I contemplated future job opportunities. I was really enjoying my classes and professors. To help cover my tuition and expenses, I was offered the opportunity to teach Introduction to Chemistry labs. It was an opportunity to learn a new skill and help others learn about a subject I enjoyed and was the basis of my degree. In my first semester, I had a far more significant learning experience, but only upon reflection in hindsight.

After each lab session, each student was required to submit a written report outlining the lab procedure and results. There were guidelines in terms of grading with respect to neatness, actual results versus theoretical yield, and timeliness, including a deduction for late submittals, 20 points for each day. Early in the semester, I had an international student who was struggling to understand the instructions and procedures. They were trying their best but still struggled. Mid-semester, the student turned in an incomplete report two days late. After following the grading rubric, the student received a grade of 68. Applying the deduction for the late submittal, the final grade was a 28. My fellow lab instructors wondered how I could give that score. In my mind, I was doing as I had been instructed and wouldn't bend. In hindsight, I missed an opportunity to better understand the struggles of someone else and help them improve. It would take me several years to fully comprehend the value of helping others (but more on that later).

(BELATED) LEARNING POINT – Helping others improve and succeed isn't a sign of weakness. In fact, it is a sign of strength.

A NEW DIRECTION

In addition to my studies and my job teaching chemistry labs, I interviewed with some other companies for summer internships. One day after finishing my own labs, when I got back to my apartment, I had a voice message on my answering machine (side note: there were no emails or cell phones in the fall of 1981). The message was from Shell offering me a summer job in their New Orleans office as a reservoir engineer. I heard "office" and "New Orleans" (which weren't "plant" and "East Texas") and got very excited about the offer. The next morning, while getting my breakfast from the student lounge (Snickers and a Coke, the breakfast of champions, or at least the breakfast of a hurried, lazy junior), I asked my classmates what a reservoir engineer did. They didn't know and told me to ask some of the petroleum engineering students. Since I didn't know anyone in the petroleum engineering department, I took a chance and accepted the offer. I didn't really know what the job would be, but I did know that it wasn't working in a chemical plant in East Texas. Who knew that this was the start to an exciting and adventure-filled career?

I moved to New Orleans in the summer of 1982 for my internship with Shell Oil Company. I learned that I would be working with a group of reservoir engineers and working on a field in the shallow waters of the Gulf of Mexico, or GoM (as it was called then). I still didn't know what a reservoir engineer did, but I was eager to find out. My mentor was a more experienced engineer. He was a patient individual, always willing to answer my many questions and offer advice and guidance. My job that summer was to evaluate the performance of a field in the GoM producing through a waterflood. I was supposed to make recommendations on how to improve the overall production of the wells and increase the oil recovery from those wells. After two weeks, I knew I had found my career. A burden of uncertainty was lifted from my shoulders. I had always liked puzzles and solving problems (remember, I was still that "nerd" from high school). In my internship, I was intrigued by the task of understanding how the field was performing based on the daily reports from the wells. It was like solving a really big 3-dimensional puzzle. My job was finding the right connections.

By the end of the summer, I had learned a little bit about what being a reservoir engineer meant. It wasn't just a job. It was fun (and I was getting paid).

I eagerly approached each day, trying to learn all I could about my field and trying to figure out solutions for improved performance. At the end of the summer, I gave my recommendations to my mentor and the team. They were warmly received. During my final week, the manager of the group offered me a full-time position upon graduation. I returned to campus both elated and a little nervous.

LEARNING POINT – When new opportunities arise, don't be afraid to step out of your comfort zone. Remember, it is a chance to learn and grow. And when you find something you like to do, it's no longer work. It becomes a passion and a joy.

I returned to campus ready to complete my senior year, graduate, and return to New Orleans to work for Shell. On the last day of my internship, my mentor jokingly said that since I had a job in hand, I had better watch out, as I might meet a young lady during my last year. I laughed since I was not dating anyone. Who knew that two weeks into the semester, I would meet my future wife? My roommates did tease me about the fact that she was a freshman, and I was a senior. [And 41 years later, I am happy and blessed that she was bold enough to ask me out. And that I was smart enough to ask her to marry me.]

TRAGEDY STRIKES AND LIFE CHANGES

My final semester rolled around. The end was in sight. I was down to my final four classes. The semester was off to a great start. Then tragedy struck.

On the second weekend of the semester, the big basketball game between Mississippi State and Ole Miss was going to be played on the MSU campus at the Humphrey Coliseum (The Hump). My older sister and younger brother were going to join my girlfriend and me for the game. As the time for the game drew near, my sister showed up, but not my brother. We headed to the game and left a note for my brother to meet us there. As the game approached half-time, an announcement was made: "David Purvis, go to the ticket office for a message."

The message was for me to call home. That call would have a lasting effect on my life. When I called, one of the deacons from our local church answered. I knew something was wrong. He told me that my brother had been killed in an accident with a drunk driver on his way to campus to go to the game. What a shock and a devastating blow. After going back to our seats,

34

my sister and I went back to my apartment. We packed our bags, went to pick up my girlfriend, and drove to Meridian, arriving to find a house full of grief. It created a hole in the hearts of my parents for the rest of their lives. For me, it put a pall on my last few months at school. I quickly learned to lean on my faith, family, and friends. I returned to campus with a drive to take my studies and relationships to a new level.

While sad on the one hand, I still looked forward to the end of the semester and graduation. The year ended well, and I graduated Summa Cum Laude with a 3.97 GPA (that dang B in Honors Calculus II).

LEARNING POINT – Life can change suddenly. Pursue the things you love, both in your work and your life.

The years finishing high school and at MSU brought me many lessons that would become the foundation for a life of learning and growing my leadership capabilities. With graduation behind me and my degree in hand, I was ready to head to New Orleans and begin my work as a reservoir engineer for Shell Oil Company.

Back to the question I asked at the beginning of the chapter: What do you do when you don't fit the definition of normal? After four years of university study, a couple of internships, growing up, and stepping out of my comfort zone to become more outgoing and vocal, my answer was: Be confident, be yourself, and grow your capabilities. You will find the best spot to start growing your tree.

++++++++++++++++++++

Over this chapter, I have shared the lessons I learned while planting the seed of my career. For those at this stage, you should start:

- Building your personal and professional network
- Testing your career options through shadowing, internships, and part-time jobs to help you determine what you like/love to do
- Continue learning to help fertilize your growing Career Tree
- Stepping out of your comfort zone to grow your skills and build resiliency.

REFLECTION QUESTIONS:

- Where are my areas of complacency, and what am I doing to challenge myself to grow?
- Do I know what I like to do and don't like to do to help me decide where to plant my tree? If not, what am I doing to test my options?
- What is something new I learned today?
- How did I express my joy today?

SUMMARY OF LEARNINGS – MY EARLY YEARS

- Don't be complacent. Just because you are GOOD doesn't mean you can't get BETTER. Never stop learning and growing your skills.
- You can always learn something from everyone you encounter. You just have to be willing to accept the lesson.
- You can't grow by staying in your comfort zone. Without pushing your limits, you become self-limiting.
- Success rarely comes overnight. Success is gained by learning from each effort, taking feedback, and

incorporating improvement tips. Many times, success is built by many small steps, improving one on the other.

- REPEAT – Don't be complacent. Just because you are GOOD doesn't mean you can't get BETTER. Never stop learning and growing your skills.
- Don't become overly focused on one element. Strive for balance in school, work, family, friends, and faith.
- It doesn't matter if your job is as a professional, tradesman, or in the service sector. Hard work creates value for others.
- Knowing what you don't want/like to do is as important as knowing what you love to do.
- (BELATED) Helping others improve and succeed isn't a sign of weakness. In fact, it is a sign of strength.
- When new opportunities arise, don't be afraid to step out of your comfort zone. Remember, it is a chance to learn and grow. And when you find something you like to do, it's no longer work. It becomes a passion and a joy.
- Life can change suddenly. Pursue the things you love, both in your work and your life.

Chapter 3

Growing Deep Roots and Building the Trunk – Early Career Days

Once you have planted the seed for your career, it is time to start growing your roots and building the trunk. This chapter focuses on the early years of your career. We will explore the challenges and opportunities that come as you grow your core skills, establish functional excellence, overcome hurdles, and expand your professional network. We will see the value of mentors and setting professional goals. Finally, we will see how deepening your skills and growing your Career Tree trunk can position you for future roles.

THE START OF ADULTING & LEARNING DOESN'T STOP WHEN YOU GET YOUR DEGREE

With graduation behind me, I was off to the corporate world with my new job at Shell in New Orleans. As mentioned previously, adulting, here I come. Who knew the transition could be so hard?

I was in for some rude awakenings, and I mean literally. University students often complain about having to wake up for 8 a.m. classes. When I started work, I would have already been at my desk for at least an hour if I was onshore in the office. If I was offshore, the day started with a 5 a.m. wakeup call. Either way, it meant early starts to my day. And training didn't end with my university degree. Shell ran its own training center in Houston. I had classes totaling almost 3 months during my first year of work. By class, I meant learning from an in-house (and industry) expert from 8 to 5 every day for a couple of weeks at a time. The subjects included Reservoir Engineering, Formation Evaluation, Structural Geology, Production Engineering, Wells, and Oil and Gas Economics. Each class was like cramming a full semester of university into two weeks.

And it wasn't just sitting and listening. We were tested each week. At the end of each course, your results were reported back to your supervisor and manager. The stakes were high. As a non-petroleum engineer, I often felt like I was behind the curve. I sometimes felt like I had Impostor Syndrome and worried that my bosses would find out I wasn't really qualified to be a reservoir engineer. I wanted to make sure I had learned my lessons from high school and University and not rest on my perceived knowledge and understanding of a topic. I hit the books. *Hard.* I wanted to apply my new knowledge in helping understand and improve the performance of the oil and gas fields I was working on. In the end, I wanted to be among the best in my craft (reservoir engineering).

LEARNING POINT – When starting something new (job, craft, adventure), put in the extra effort to learn the fundamentals and be the best you can be.

MY FIRST TEST

With my initial training complete, it was now time to start practicing my craft. One of my first assignments was as an offshore field engineer. Our primary role was to ensure we obtained high-quality data from the wells we were drilling, particularly for exploration wells looking for new oil and gas fields. Since our time was the cheapest part of the well, we were often sent offshore days before we were required to be on site. This could mean a couple of days spent doing nothing more than reading or watching TV. I quickly learned that I liked to travel by helicopter versus boat, but I didn't get a vote on the mode of transportation.

A key area of emphasis for the company was employee and job safety. One example stands out in my mind that highlights this focus. After spending 10 days offshore on a job with many nights spent providing quality assurance for the logging activities, I arrived back at the shore base. As I was retrieving my luggage, the logistics coordinator handed me a note telling me to call my boss about an urgent matter. (Reminder to all, in the fall of 1983, there were no cell phones, so yes, a note from the heliport staff was the equivalent of a text message.)

When I called in, my boss said I needed to get back on the next helicopter and head to another platform to supervise a complex job on an important well. He said I was the closest team member available, and the rig was waiting on someone from our team to arrive so the job could proceed. I was conflicted. I had been with the company for less than a year, but I was *exhausted*. I took a chance and explained it to my boss. I raised the point that I had been up for several nights in a row with minimal sleep. I also expressed concern that, given the complexity of the upcoming job, which I had never performed before, there was a high risk of an unsuccessful attempt, with the potential for large expenses for the company. After hearing my concerns, my boss agreed with my views and agreed to deploy another teammate to the job. In the end, it was the right call. I collapsed when I got back home and slept for over 12 hours, and the teammate who went on the job was more experienced and delivered a successful outcome.

LEARNING POINT – Don't be afraid to speak up when you feel a request/directive is unethical, immoral, or unsafe or will put you, others, or the company at risk. And if you are the boss, be willing to listen to the input of your staff. Safety should never be compromised for expediency.

EARLY TECHNICAL PROGRESS

Over the next few years, I had a variety of reservoir engineering roles. Early jobs included evaluating the performance of producing fields to improve their performance. These roles provided me with the opportunity to grow my technical skills as a reservoir engineer. One of my key learnings in those early years was the value of my teammates. There were three other primary members of our team. Together, we worked on several fields in the Gulf of Mexico. As the early-career reservoir engineer, I focused on well and field performance. The late-career geologist understood the structural characteristics of the reservoir and field. The mid-career production engineer focused on the producing wells, and the mid-career facilities engineer focused on the topside processing equipment. While we were each good at our individual crafts, working together, we became a formidable team and increased production from several older oil and gas fields, significantly extending their production life and value to the company.

LEARNING POINT – Being good at your craft is the starting point. Working closely with others who are good at their jobs leads to outstanding results. To achieve outstanding results, you must be willing to lean on others for support in unfamiliar areas.

GAINING A MENTOR (OR TWO)

Over the course of my training classes and work assignments, I worked hard to overcome the Impostor Syndrome I felt on occasion. Our instructors had encouraged us to find a mentor. The question for me was who? As luck would have it, I had two right at hand without realizing it.

In my early technical assignments, I was working on multiple fields in the Gulf of Mexico. Three of the fields had the same geologist, a very experienced man who had been an industry leader in advancing Shell and the industry into deeper-water developments. He was extremely knowledgeable and encouraged me to learn more about other technical disciplines beyond my own area of specialty. To emphasize this approach, he often challenged me to draw my own maps and estimate the hydrocarbon volumes in the reservoir. While some of my colleagues argued that this work was technically his responsibility, I saw it as real "on-the-job" training that helped me strengthen my understanding of subsurface settings and gain confidence in my skills. I was quickly learning about an integrated multi-disciplinary approach to solving problems, which went beyond the classroom training I had recently completed. In hindsight, this was a great accelerator for building my technical skills.

At the same time, this individual was known for his unorthodox interactions with senior leadership, challenging leaders who didn't appreciate or understand the technical aspects of a field or the basis for recommended actions to bring on new oil production. In fact, my supervisor and manager both encouraged me to limit my time with this individual. They felt he would give me bad guidance on dealing with others. In my naivete, I asked how I could limit my time since he was the primary geologist for most of my fields, and my performance goals called for me to work closely with the other disciplines to improve field performance. I tried to reassure my bosses that I would only focus on the technical elements in my interactions.

Luckily, the geologist on my other field was a well-regarded mid-career female. She encouraged me to do the same technical analysis as the experienced geologist. In fact, he had been her technical mentor when she joined Shell. In contrast to her colleague, this individual was well-regarded for her interactions with people at all levels. She taught me to ask questions of others, seek to learn more about where they did not understand an issue, and focus on improving my communication skills to ensure my technical analysis and recommendations were clear, concise, and well understood by others. I credit her with helping me develop my engagement and interaction skills and helping me get out of my introverted shell.

During my early assignments, I was blessed to have these two individuals take time to help improve my skills. They demonstrated the value of serving as a mentor and investing in developing others. Looking forward, I credit both individuals for instilling in me a sense of purpose to help others grow. I continued the practice of having a mentor at each level of my career and also became a mentor as I moved into my mid-career and late-career roles.

LEARNING POINT – As you grow your capabilities, be sure to seek out a mentor to help you develop further. They are a great resource for expanding your knowledge, giving advice, broadening your perspective, and becoming a better you, both technically and personally.

BROADENING MY SKILLS AND HORIZONS

Who knew how important teamwork was going to be in my next assignment? The more I interacted with the production engineers for my fields, the more I was interested in better understanding the wells. Luckily, one of the production engineers had a similar interest. We went to our bosses and arranged a job swap. This was a unique proposal, and amazingly, our bosses agreed. After 4+ years as a reservoir engineer, this was the start of my 15-month broadening assignment, a chance to broaden my technical skills beyond my core specialty.

The main deliverable from this Production Engineering assignment was to design and execute a "workover" program to correct some problems with a handful of wells on an older platform. One well needed the production tubing replaced due to a deep hole. This was a problem that had been identified several months earlier and was being actively managed to minimize the well integrity risk until the rig arrived at the platform to repair the damage. A few other wells had small changes to improve production performance. I was excited about the opportunity as it fit with my natural desire to learn new topics. I had no idea of the changes that were coming my way.

LEARNING POINT – Don't pass up an opportunity to challenge yourself, broaden your skill set, and grow your capabilities. This includes self-study, classes, formal training, or on-the-job training.

I spent the first three weeks in my new assignment working out the details for the upcoming rig program. The start date was getting close, with the rig about a week away from arriving on site, when I got a call on the weekend from the field supervisor on the platform. He said that there were "bubbles" in the water around the platform. We couldn't understand what was causing it. We thought it might be a leak from the gas pipeline. The field had been shut down the previous week to perform a repair on the pipeline. The field had just returned to production a couple of days before. With safety in mind, we agreed to shut in the field and blow down the gas pipeline to ensure there wasn't another leak.

A couple of hours later, the field supervisor called me back and said that the bubbles were getting bigger. If it was another pipeline leak, bigger bubbles didn't make any sense. From my freshman chemistry, I'd learned that, with the pressure and gas volume in the pipeline decreasing, the bubbles should have been getting smaller. The field team started checking the pressure gauges on all wells. One well was acting strangely, and we thought we might have an underground blowout in one of the wells on the platform. The offshore team quickly began securing the other 17 wells on the platform and preparing to abandon the location due to the increasing bubbles and natural gas around the platform.

The next morning, I met with the senior operations leaders in the office to plan the path forward. To my amazement (and if I admit it, my bewilderment), they looked at me and said that, as the production engineer, I needed to take the lead in figuring out what had happened, which wells were involved, and if there was going to be any lasting impact on the other wells. In my mind, the impostor syndrome kicked in. Inside, I was shouting, "I'm not an expert! I'm just playing at being a production engineer, and I've only been doing that for about a month! I have no idea what has happened." Outside, I said, "Yes, sir," and got after it. After talking to the field supervisor and a quick review of the pressure data from each of the wells, we concluded that the culprit was the well with the hole in the tubing, the primary driver for the upcoming rig program. **We had been one week too late.**

The field teams took the lead in securing the wells and platform, bringing in specialty vessels and equipment to pump mud into all the wells, including the blowout well. This shut off the gas and water flow from under the platform but also damaged the platform structure due to the shifting soil underneath the pilings. For my part, I reached out to my teammates in my prior role, particularly the geologist (a 30+ year expert) and the production engineer who had worked in the field previously (and swapped jobs with me). We started reviewing the data and confirmed the culprit well.

Over the next several months, while the platform was being repaired, we collected additional information on all the other wells and ultimately determined that three or four wells had been damaged beyond repair and would need to be safely abandoned once the platform was repaired and a rig was brought in. I continued reviewing the data being collected and had concerns that we had not fully resolved the blowout, primarily based on the measured temperature about 500 feet below the seabed under the platform. Some recent logs had shown that the temperature was still elevated above the background. I tested my ideas with my teammates, who challenged my thoughts and helped me shape my conclusions and recommendations to senior management.

As we were bringing most of the wells back to production, I had proposed one last unconventional test to confirm my suspicions. I wanted to place a sensitive microphone in the blowout well around the depth of its shallowest leak point. Sitting on the platform with everything shut down to minimize outside noise and headphones on my head, my worst fears were confirmed. All I could hear was a gurgling sound, indicating that the damaged well was still slowly leaking water from the reservoir into the leak path under the platform. While disappointed, this set the teams on a path to execute a phenomenal feat of drilling a relief well to intercept the damaged well over 10,000' below the seabed and pump cement directly into the damaged well just above the blowout zone. I gladly turned this task over to the experts in drilling and completions, who did an excellent job. Once the intercept well was completed, we confirmed that the gurgling had stopped.

Finally, after 15+ months, the problem had been solved, and my broadening assignment was complete. Who knew that my "broadening assignment" to expand my skill set would be this challenging and offer me a chance to truly expand my capabilities, broaden my horizons, and build my confidence? Now, to return to my core discipline of reservoir engineering.

LEARNING POINT – When challenged and feeling overwhelmed, don't feel you have to do things by yourself. Seek out others for advice, guidance, and support. Working together, you can address the challenges at hand.

GETTING MY LICENSE

After wrapping up my broadening assignment and moving back to a subsurface team, I also took the opportunity to take the exam for my Professional Engineering (PE) license. At that time, you had to have at least 4 years of technical experience and have recommendations from current professional engineers. But I faced a dilemma. My degree was in chemical engineering, but I had not done any practical work in that area since graduating from Mississippi State University. Not only did I not have the experience, but I would also not be able to get any truthful recommendations. So, this meant taking the PE exam in petroleum engineering. I still felt a bit of Impostor Syndrome as this wasn't the area of my university degree, but it was what I had been doing for the past five years. The PE license wasn't required for my job. I wanted to get it for personal satisfaction and for future consideration. I spent the next several months building my confidence by studying, doing practice problems, and taking mock exams at night.

On the day of the exam, I brought my study guides, key textbooks, and industry handbooks into the exam room. Over the next eight hours, I would spend my time picking out eight problems to answer (out of 20 choices). With a quick read of the morning slate of problems, I quickly realized that there were not enough reservoir engineering-based questions to meet the required 4 problems. The afternoon session was the same, with not enough reservoir engineering-based questions to meet the required four problems to be answered. Thankfully, in each session, there were a couple of questions that I could answer based on my well work experience from my broadening assignment. I took a moment to be thankful for both asking for that opportunity and for all the experts who had helped me grow my skills. To be successful in getting my PE license, I was going to have to demonstrate and prove the breadth of my technical skills.

At the end of the testing day, I was mentally and physically exhausted. Now it was just a matter of waiting for the results to be graded and seeing if I passed. The national pass rate was less than 60%. I felt good, but you never know. As the weeks passed, I was involved in the work for my new team but also anxious to see the results. When I got home from work one day, my wife handed me a letter. With some hesitation, I tore it open and read the results. I HAD PASSED. I was now a licensed Professional Engineer in petroleum engineering. My wife just laughed. She said she knew I had passed by the way the letter was addressed. I said what? She said to take another look at the letter. When I did, I saw that it was addressed to David Purvis, PE. Ha.

When I spoke to some colleagues at work, I was one of the few who had passed. On reflection, I realized that each of them was very good at their core skill but didn't have the breadth of knowledge of the various aspects of the petroleum industry that the PE license tested. I encouraged them to take the test again and, this time, study areas adjacent to their core discipline to gain the breadth of knowledge needed to answer additional questions on the exam. Many of them passed on their next try.

LEARNING POINT – While it may not be required for your job, setting and achieving goals for personal development and industry recognition are great motivators.

REPEAT LEARNING POINT – Don't pass up an opportunity to challenge yourself, broaden your skill set, and grow your capabilities. You never know when those skills may be needed.

DEEPENING MY CORE SKILLS

With my broadening assignment complete (and the blowout field returning to production), my next reservoir engineering role was with the team supporting the new emerging area of deepwater development with Tension Leg Platforms (TLPs). These types of developments had never been done before in the oil and gas industry, so the chance to work in this exciting field was an honor. Being a part of cutting-edge technology was exciting.

My early assignments were supporting senior engineers in the design, modeling, and economic evaluation of the first deepwater project in the Gulf of Mexico, named Auger. This was a great opportunity to deepen my technical skills in my core discipline. While I primarily focused on the project's economic modeling, I got an early taste of the numerical modeling and risk assessment needed to ensure the technical, operational, and financial risks of a large-scale project were well understood and addressed.

LEARNING POINT – If given the opportunity to learn from an expert, take full advantage of their experience and expertise. Ask questions, seek feedback, soak up their knowledge.

Over the next few years, I was given some choice assignments on key fields over some more experienced colleagues. I also received my first merit-based promotion a year earlier than most of my workmates. As a result, I let my early success go to my head and became arrogant and a bit of a jerk (based on feedback from some work colleagues and my best supporter – my wife). This wasn't my intention, but it was how I came across to others. With this feedback, I vowed to be more engaging and less irritating.

LEARNING POINT – As you build your skills and achieve levels of success, be humble. Your success is more than the result of just your personal skills. The support from others very likely plays an important part in your success.

Subsequent assignments included being involved in the early evaluation of the next major deepwater discovery and being the lead engineer on the design on a later deepwater development. Both these projects had industry partners, which gave me a great opportunity to learn the art of negotiating.

On the deepwater development project, the other partners were also major players in the industry and had their top technical staff assigned to the design teams. Reaching an agreement on critical field design elements was a challenge. This is where a recent training class paid off. We studied the recent book by Stephen R. Covey, *The 7 Habits of Highly Effective People*. Rather than get confrontational about design differences between the various companies, I thought about

Habit 4 – "Think Win-Win" and Habit 5 – "Seek first to understand, then to be understood." This allowed the companies to align on the best design based on input from all the teams.

Rather than force our preferred design on the partners, we held several workshops where each company shared its design concepts for the field development, including the number of wells, facility size, and oil recovery methods. After the workshops, the project leads from each team met to review the proposals. In the end, we agreed on a final design that incorporated elements from all the partners and was better than any single proposal.

LEARNING POINT – When faced with differences of opinion (whether technical, financial, operational, or strategic), keep in mind the advice from Covey's 7 Habits of Highly Effective People: Habit 4 – Think Win-Win and Habit 5 – Seek first to understand, then to be understood.

EXPANDING MY SKILL SET – FIELD TRIP

With my return to the subsurface reservoir engineering team working on the emerging deepwater area, we were encouraged to learn more about the geological deposition of the reservoirs to improve our understanding of the continuity of the sands and their impact on performance and well spacing. I was lucky enough to land a spot in one of the prime internal courses. It would consist of a week in class in Houston, followed by field work in Arkansas and then California.

When I described the class to my wife and friends outside of the industry, they all said I was going on a "boondoggle." As defined by Webster's New Collegiate Dictionary (the one on my desk at the time of my trip), a "boondoggle" is a "trivial, useless, or wasteful project or activity." I think they meant it was going to be a company-paid vacation to walk in the country in Arkansas and on the beaches of California.

Boy, were they wrong. The class was taught by the company's geology gurus. The majority of the participants were in disciplines other than geology or geophysics. Some had previously taken some geology classes at university. And some (including me) knew our geologist by name, but that was about it. The work was intense (think a university semester class crammed into a week of 8 to 5 classroom time). My brain was about to explode. Then we headed to the field. Now the fun part was about to start. *Not!* We arrived outside Fort Smith, Arkansas, in the middle of the summer. We took buses out to the start of the area to study and hiked to a large open area. It was hot, steamy, and thick with mosquitoes. The instructors pointed to a ridge line, 300 or 400 yards away, that extended for about half a mile. Our assignment: map out the geological layers we saw in the opposite rock face. *What????*

Those with some geology background jumped in. Shoot, some of them even had their own colored pencils. The non-geo group stood back, wondering where to start. I think the instructors took pity on us (me). They started asking questions about what we saw. They pointed out some landmarks. As I calmed down and started dissecting the rock face in front of me, my picture began to take shape. In the end, even though my cross-section wasn't as detailed or as fancy as the more experienced participants', it was still a pretty good representation of what I saw.

The next step was to fly to San Diego, California. The course called for the group to study some outcrops. The best viewpoint just happened to be from the beach. And the beach in question just happened to be Blacks Beach in La Jolla, California. If you're not familiar, Blacks Beach is a famous "nude" beach. As we pulled into the bus parking lot, the instructors were very insistent that we present ourselves as a geology study group, not as oil and gas professionals from a major oil company. We had been instructed not to wear any gear or clothing that had the company logo. (Remember, this is California in the late 1980s, as the environmental movement was gaining steam.) The group headed down to the beach and started walking along the outcrop. It just so happened that the best view of the outcrop was by walking along the waterline. There were a couple of times when the instructors told us to make sure we were looking at the rocks, not the sunbathers. Hmmm, maybe the "boondoggle" comment had some validity. As we flew back to Houston, I reflected on what I had learned from the three parts of the class (classroom and two field visits). While I would never compete as a geologist, I could now start thinking about my reservoir engineering assessments with a geological mindset.

LEARNING POINT – When a learning opportunity presents itself, don't let it be a "boondoggle," a trivial or useless activity. Make sure you focus and use the time to build your skills, broaden your perspective, and deepen your capabilities.

MOVING ON (IN MORE WAYS THAN ONE)

After a couple of years working on the development plans for the new horizons of deepwater oil and gas fields, I requested a transfer to another area of advanced technology in the industry, enhanced oil recovery via CO_2 flooding. I was going to be the working supervisor for a team of engineers. Not only was it moving to a new team, but it also meant moving to a new city: Houston, Texas. We found out about the move on August 2, 1990. It was quite an evening of watching the news of Iraq's invasion of Kuwait while contemplating moving to a new city, restarting our home, finding new friends, and joining a new team.

Per my own career tree, after seven years, I had grown deep and solid roots and built a solid trunk. I was now moving into my mid-career segment. It was time to start branching out.

++++++++++++++++++++

Over this chapter, we have seen the lessons I learned while growing deep roots and building a strong trunk for my career. For those at this stage, you should start:

- Expanding your personal and professional network
- Deepening your functional skills
- Connecting with peers in adjacent disciplines and learn how the work they do connects with your focus area
- Challenging yourself to demonstrate proficiency
- Finding a mentor (or two) to help you grow your functional skills and interpersonal skills
- Building a reputation for quality work and dependability

REFLECTION QUESTIONS:

- Am I recognized by my peers and colleagues for my functional skills? If not, where are my areas of weakness?
- What am I doing to strengthen my functional skills?
- Do I have a mentor (both personal and professional)? If not, who can I ask to help me grow my trunk?
- What am I doing to improve my communication skills, written and verbal?
- What am I learning about other areas outside of my core functional skill set?

SUMMARY OF LEARNING POINTS – EARLY CAREER GROWING MY ROOTS AND BUILDING MY TRUNK

- When starting something new (job, craft, adventure), put in the extra effort to learn the fundamentals and be the best you can be.
- Don't be afraid to speak up when you feel a request/directive is unethical, immoral, or unsafe or will put you, others, or the company at risk. And if you are the boss, be willing to listen to the input of your staff. Safety should never be compromised for expediency.
- Being good at your craft is the starting point. Working closely with others who are good at their jobs leads to outstanding results. To achieve outstanding results, you must be willing to lean on others for support in unfamiliar areas.
- As you grow your capabilities, be sure to seek out a mentor to help you develop further. They are a great resource for expanding your knowledge, giving advice, broadening your

perspective, and becoming a better you, both technically and personally.

- Don't pass up an opportunity to challenge yourself, broaden your skill set, and grow your capabilities. This includes self-study, classes, formal training, or on-the-job training.
- When challenged and feeling overwhelmed, don't feel you have to do things by yourself. Seek out others for advice, guidance, and support. Working together, you can address the challenges at hand.
- While it may not be required for your job, setting and achieving goals for personal development and industry recognition are great motivators.
- REPEAT– Don't pass up an opportunity to challenge yourself, broaden your skill set, and grow your capabilities. You never know when those skills may be needed.
- If given the opportunity to learn from an expert, take full advantage of their experience and expertise. Ask questions, seek feedback, soak up their knowledge.
- As you build your skills and achieve levels of success, be humble. Your success is more than the result of just your personal skills. The support from others very likely plays an important part in your success.
- When faced with differences of opinion (whether technical, financial, operational, or strategic), keep in mind the advice from Covey's *7 Habits of Highly Effective People*: Habit 4 – Think Win-Win and Habit 5 – Seek first to understand, then to be understood.
- When a learning opportunity presents itself, don't let it be a "boondoggle," a trivial or useless activity. Make sure you focus and use the time to build your skills, broaden your perspective, and deepen your capabilities.

Mid-Career

Branching Out

Chapter 4

Mid-Career – Branching out to New Challenges – Leadership Roles

Having planted the seed of your career and invested time in growing your skills to grow a solid trunk, now is the time to branch out. This chapter focuses on the transition to mid-career. During this period, I had my first supervisory role, undertook business-planning roles to develop non-technical skills, secured my first direct field operations leadership role, and completed a special assignment leveraging my technical and business skills.

We will explore the challenges and opportunities that come with taking on roles outside your core discipline, advancing towards becoming a technical expert, and moving into supervisory roles, taking on the accountability of developing others and delivering performance for the whole team, not just yourself.

FIRST SUPERVISOR ROLE – SO MUCH TO LEARN

With the move to Houston, I took on the role of working supervisor for the Eastern CO_2 floods in Mississippi and Louisiana. I was leading a group of other reservoir engineers who were working to optimize the performance of the fields in

Mississippi and finalize the design of the CO_2 flood in Louisiana.

Including myself, we were a team of four. We were a small group, but it was the start of my leadership journey. The job brought its own challenges. In addition to my own work of reviewing the performance of one of the fields, I also had to guide and review the work of the other team members. Striking that balance was difficult at the start. The transition from an individual contributor to a supervisor came with some challenges. The primary responsibility as the supervisor was no longer doing the work but ensuring quality work was being done by the other team members. I quickly learned that my job wasn't to do their work for them nor to double-check their work. I found my comfort zone when I took the time to learn each team member's strengths and areas for improvement. Together, we established a routine of discussing monthly objectives and deliverables, followed by weekly check-ins to review the most recent results of the CO_2 injection modifications we were implementing. I also learned to give other team members opportunities to develop their work-planning skills, in addition to building their technical skills. I think that at the end of the year, we had all grown in our capabilities.

LEARNING POINT – As a supervisor, your success is dependent on the success of the individual team members. Knowing their strengths, areas of improvement, and building a sense of collective ownership is a foundation for success.

REPEAT LEARNING POINT – Helping others improve and succeed isn't a sign of weakness. In fact, it is a sign of strength.

KNOWING WHEN TO SAY NO

After the team's success in improving the performance of the smaller CO_2 floods in Mississippi, I undertook a new role as the lead engineer for an expansion of a CO_2 flood in onshore South Louisiana. The field had been injecting CO_2 for several years, and the decision point for drilling the producing wells was approaching. This was going to be a significant investment of several hundred million dollars (in 1991, or over $500 million in 2025).

The team included a reservoir engineer, a production engineer, a facilities engineer, a petrophysical engineer, and a geologist. We all had 8 to 15 years of experience (mid-career level). In our initial meeting, we outlined the key deliverables and objectives of the project. Key amongst them was to determine the number of wells needed and the best place to drill them. The project had been injecting CO_2 for several years already, sourced from the Jackson Dome CO_2 field near Jackson, MS, and transported through a dedicated CO_2 pipeline. The original design of the project, based on the field trial and computer modeling, indicated that an oil bank should be present. We just needed to confirm the presence of the oil bank and then spot the well locations for the drilling team to execute. It all sounded so simple. Little did we know.

The petrophysical engineer took the lead on scheduling the logs, working with the production engineer to get access to the wells in what we thought was the best location to spot the oil bank. A couple of weeks later, the petrophysical engineer called us to come by his office. He sounded very worried. We hurried down to his office. His first words were, "It's not there."

I said, "What?"

He repeated, "It's not there. There's no oil bank."

How could that be? Our company's experts designed the project, conducted a field trial in the reservoir next to the full project, signed off on the pipeline investment, and injected CO_2 into the target reservoir for several years. How could it be wrong?

Not wanting to sound the alarm, I took the information back to my office and began researching the basis for the initial project approval, reviewing the field trial results, evaluating the surrounding reservoirs, and modeling CO_2 injection in oil reservoirs. I did alert my manager that the initial logs were disappointing and that I was reviewing the results to develop a recommended path forward. In other words, I was hedging my bets on the downside before I knew more. As I dug further into the historical data and built my models, I found a select few late-career experts in my discipline, in addition to my teammates, whom I could show my results and test my ideas.

REPEAT LEARNING POINT – When challenged and feeling overwhelmed, don't feel you have to do things by yourself. Seek out others for advice, guidance, and support. Working together, you can address the challenges at hand.

Ultimately, after many anxious moments, I concluded that the initial analysis had overestimated the amount of oil that could be recovered and that the field trial was not a good analog for the final project. In other words, the initial investment had been made on a flawed design and would not recover sufficient volume to pay off the investment.

The team reviewed the analysis and agreed on the findings. Needless to say, we did not recommend further investment. In fact, we recommended stopping the project, even though we had already invested several hundred million dollars. We shared the outcome with our managers, who were shocked by the results. Before agreeing to stop the project, they asked the team to verify the results with a field test. We were supposed to figure out how to take an existing well, produce from the measured CO_2 bank, and confirm that the oil present was not sufficient for further investment. NO BIG DEAL (even though it had not been done before).

At this point, the team rallied around the challenge. We all started working on our individual segments of the design for the field test. I had the easiest portion of modeling various outcomes of percent oil present. The toughest jobs were for the production engineer and facilities engineer. The production engineer had to figure out how to use an old well to do a field test. The facilities engineer had to figure out how to lay a temporary flowline and find a big enough heater to allow the production of the high CO_2 volumes we expected without freezing the test equipment.

A month or so later, it all came together, and we journeyed from Houston to South Louisiana to run the field test. It was both exciting and nerve-racking. What if we were wrong? This was a real test of our technical skills. We all stood by anxiously as the well started producing. The first thing we noticed was that the choke on the manifold was starting to freeze. This was our indication of a high CO_2 content. We continued to monitor the results for most of the day. The initial estimates from the field were right in line with our best estimate. I confirmed the results when I got back to the office. The target reservoir had almost 50% less oil volume as a target than estimated from the initial project design.

Our management team agreed with the results from the field trial. They asked us for one final review with the most senior experts in each of our respective fields. Together, the team assembled the data, our analysis, the well test results, and final conclusions (including the errors in the original project design) and recommendations. After gaining the support of the experts, we had to present the findings and recommendations to the senior management team. This was my first real engagement with the executive team. *No big deal*, except that one of the executives had been a member of the original design team for the project. I was going to have to tell him that the original design team was wrong.

On the day of the project review, I was sweating bullets. I had never really been nervous in presentations before, but this was a whole different level. The team presented our results and feedback from the review with the expert panel. At the end, the executive team thanked us for a thorough review and endorsed our recommendation to halt the project. We had saved the company from investing several hundred million additional dollars in a doomed project. In fact, the team members won the President's Award for Technical Excellence the following year.

LEARNING POINT – Stopping a bad project is just as important as advancing a good project. Either way, you need to have a strong technical basis and thorough economic analysis for your recommendations. Let the work speak for itself.

LEARNING POINT – While building your core skills, two additional skills to work on are communication skills (both written and verbal) and financial knowledge. Being able to clearly and concisely communicate key points and demonstrate the profitability of your work will enhance your overall effectiveness.

STEPPING AWAY FROM ENGINEERING (FOR A WHILE)

Shortly after we completed the work to stop the CO_2 project in South Louisiana, my manager approached me with an opportunity to take on a new job assignment as the division planner. I would be working directly with the Vice President for Onshore US to coordinate the annual business plans from the various divisions. I would still be supervising staff but not engineers. While I had taken some business courses at university, this was a chance to learn more about the business side of our industry. The role also gave me the opportunity to learn the onshore portfolio, which had operations across the entire US. As I got started, two immediate challenges faced me. The first was learning to supervise staff whose key skills were not in my own area of expertise. The second was that the tools used to forecast future performance across the various production divisions were outdated, particularly in financial modeling.

The new team consisted of three technical assistants who had worked in the planning organization for more than 10 years and a couple of engineers who were on their own broadening assignments. As the details of the business planning process were new to me, I quickly learned that the technical assistants were a gift. They knew the ins and outs of the process and what good quality looked like. I quickly came to rely on their experience and insight.

LEARNING POINT – Just because you are the supervisor (or senior member of a team) doesn't mean you have all the answers. Learn to value and leverage the experience of your other team members.

On the second issue of an out-of-date process and forecasting tool for the 5-year and "end of life" plans, the solution came from two different directions. First, the team once again asked for the input of the technical assistants who had worked in the group for so long. They quickly identified issues raised by teams in the past and pointed out areas in the program where they had to "patch" the outcome or work offline to get a more accurate answer for the final financial performance. Second, one of the engineers on his broadening assignment had also done some computer programming.

We had just over six months to build a new program, test its viability, and roll it out to the teams to start the new process. I pitched the idea to our Planning Manager to let my team take the lead on designing a new planning program and process. The team felt we could do it quicker (and cheaper) than an outside group. The fallback was to use the old program for one more year. It was a risk, but I had confidence in the team. When we got the go-ahead, I charged the engineer to work with the technical assistants to build the new system. The goal was to have everything in place a couple of months before the start of the planning cycle, allowing time for testing and modifications as needed. The team was pumped to have the opportunity to tackle the task rather than using outside consultants.

At the same time as we were rebuilding the system, the VP asked me, as the supervisor, to provide him with a view of how the onshore organization would perform the next year. I couldn't really say, "Sorry, the system is down for the next four months," nor could we ask each of the divisions to run another forecast using the old system, as each group was already saying they spent too much time on forecasting with minimal value added.

So, what to do? I partnered with one of the technicians and began interviewing the leaders of the various divisions about their new well activity over the next 18 months, along with any major projects or operational disruptions during the same period. Once we had the data, I applied some of my reservoir engineering skills and built a forecast for each division. The technician helped me with converting production profiles to financial estimates for operating costs, capital investment, and ultimately net cash flow and net income. In a couple of weeks, we assembled an overview of each division and the onshore US as a whole. We met with the Planning Manager and VP, outlining the process and results, with the caveat that these were estimates appropriate at the macro level but not at an individual field level. Now we just had to wait to see the results from the actual full-scale planning process later that year.

While I was off doing my high-level plan, the redesign was hard at work. With the tight deadline and untested design, the team had a few squabbles but was making great progress. One of the other technicians had a great idea to test the prior year's plans on the new program to see the results. This helped both accelerate the timeline and gave the team confidence that the financial modeling was in line with past results. It also gave us more time to roll out and train the various groups.

As the time approached, it was all hands on deck. We assigned each team member as the focal point for a specific part of the organization. The divisions and field teams identified some improvement areas for the planning team to address for the next cycle, but no major changes were needed for the year of focus. In the end, we gathered the information and compiled the results, receiving positive feedback from both the divisions doing the forecasting and our ultimate customer, the VP for onshore US.

Oh, and regarding my earlier "personal" forecast, I was wrong but also right. How could that be? Well, I was wrong when we looked at each separate division, with none of my estimates of total production, net cash flow, and net income being close (<5%). Some were too high and some too low. However, when we looked at the total portfolio, I was right with my estimates for the whole organization, with each estimate being within 1 or 2% of the compiled results. And for the VP, this gave him a perspective that he could test performance at a higher level to help drive results.

LEARNING POINT – When facing a tough project (deadlines, challenging deliverables) spend the time to get alignment on expectations and final deliverables. Build on the varied skills and experience of the team members. Don't be afraid to bring different backgrounds together to solve a problem.

LEARNING POINT – When evaluating a portfolio of projects, remember that a high-level forecast is unlikely to be "accurate" at the individual component level. That said, there is confidence that the performance of the total portfolio can be reasonably predicted. The key is knowing at what level to trust the information.

MOVING TO MANAGEMENT AND FIELD OPERATIONS

After 18 months or so in my planning supervisor role, I had the opportunity to move to a manager's role. This was another branch of my mid-career journey. My new role was as the subsurface technical manager for the Central Division supporting fields in West Texas. I would be managing two teams. Both were multi-disciplinary teams made up of reservoir engineers, geologists, and petrophysicists. One team supported the ongoing field operations, and the other worked on the technical design and computer modeling for new waterfloods and CO_2 floods. Needless to say, most of my staff were more technically adept than I was.

This was also my first time managing supervisors and not directly supervising the technical staff. While the move from individual contributor to supervisor came with the challenge of guiding and reviewing the technical work of others, the move from supervisor to manager came with the challenge of setting direction, coordinating with other groups, and increased accountability for delivering timely results (budgets and deadlines).

LEARNING POINT – The move to a managerial role means growing new skills beyond your core functional skills. You have to become adept at effectively leading, coordinating, and interfacing with other teams to align and focus your teams on delivering results and working through others to get the results you want. You can no longer rely solely on your personal technical capabilities.

In addition to our General Manager, the leadership team was made up of two other technical managers (one for production engineers and another for facilities engineers and the sulfur recovery plant) and an operations manager. The other two technical managers were both engineers and a little older than me, but still in their mid-career. The operations manager was a late-career individual who had progressed through the field operations ranks.

After several months, the production engineering technical manager and I approached our GM with the request to gain some field operations experience. We proposed that we reorganize around geographic areas of the division and that each manager have technical staff (production engineers, reservoir engineers, and geologists) and field teams. In a sense, we would all be taking on broadening assignments, as each of us would have areas of responsibility that were not part of our core skill set.

Our GM was hesitant at first until we said that each leader had the additional responsibility of supporting the others in our respective areas of expertise. For me, that meant ensuring that the reservoir engineers and geologists on each team were performing quality work. Likewise, my colleagues would ensure that the production engineers and field staff on the other teams were doing quality work as well. It was a unique concept that would help us, as managers, grow our skills, add branches to our Career Trees, and position us to become better future leaders by broadening our understanding and perspective of the oil and gas industry. I think the "promise" from each of us to oversee the technical work of the other teams was the kicker that secured our GM's support. It meant some extra work for each of us, but in a sense, it brought us closer together as a leadership team.

LEARNING POINT – Helping colleagues succeed doesn't have to be bad for you. As you help others build their skills, they will do the same. Collectively, the enhanced performance across all teams will give greater success than just one segment or team doing well.

As we made the move, I started making more trips to the field to learn about the team members on the ground in West Texas. I know that my field supervisor must have been wondering what he had done wrong to get the punishment of educating this office-based reservoir engineer/manager about all things "operations." I will admit that outside of my offshore travel in my first year in the field support role and during my time on the blowout support and recovery, I had rarely traveled to the field in the subsequent years in my reservoir engineering assignments. In hindsight, that was a mistake, as I had self-limited my knowledge in a key area of our industry.

I would like to think that I was a sponge during those frequent field trips, soaking up all the knowledge my field supervisor had accumulated during his 35 years of experience. He was a kind and gentle man, generous with his time and knowledge. He encouraged me to get to know the field staff. We started holding team meetings in the field with both the engineers and field staff present. We conducted quarterly field and well reviews, during which everyone on the team contributed, and their input was captured, discussed, and valued. Over the months, we saw our whole team grow closer together. We also started seeing the performance of the fields improve. The collaboration was building a team culture of support, trust, and delivery. It wasn't about individual success. It was about team success. Over the next year, each field did better than it had in the past years, and the team was able to get a brand-new CO_2 flood approved for startup. And I even learned to enjoy my trips to the field, driving down dusty roads around Denver City, Texas.

LEARNING POINT – Team culture can't be demanded. Like trust, it has to be built on solid relationships and the belief that everyone is aligned on the shared objectives and will give their all for the team to succeed. Aligned goals and trust drive team success, not individual superstars.

As my first year as a technical/operations manager was drawing to a close, our senior leadership brought forward a project to form a joint venture with another major player in the region. The two companies shared working interest in many of the fields in the area but also had some big fields where only one company was involved. The belief was that a combined company focused on West Texas and New Mexico would have technical and operational advantages over other companies in the area. I was asked to lead the technical assessment teams for Shell. While I would be relying heavily on my technical reservoir engineering skills for volume assessments and my planning skills for assessing field value, I would be branching out by engaging with technical teams from other companies, creating data rooms for sharing information, and advising our senior leaders on valuations and negotiation points. I was excited for the opportunity.

Over the next several months, the technical teams from both companies shared information on field performance and financial results and conducted field visits to check on wells and facilities for asset integrity and potential safety issues. Our technical team was busy churning through our analysis of each field. We were working towards an agreed deadline to share the value of each field in the portfolio and the proposed split of ownership in the new merged company. But we hit a snag, a major one. No matter how we crunched the numbers, the two sides remained more than 15% apart in their proposed split of the company. We thought it should be 40/60, and they thought it should be 25/75. Internally, our leadership said that it was too big a gap to negotiate. Frustrations were growing.

My VP encouraged me to reexamine the entire analysis. I came back a couple of days later with the following insights:

1) Where both companies had an interest in a given field, the value assigned to the field by each company was very close, generally within 1 or 2% of each other, and when looking at the whole portfolio of common interest fields, less than 1% difference.

2) Where we were the only ones with an interest in a given field, our value was generally significantly higher than the other company's value for the field, often 50% or more higher.

3) Where they were the only ones with an interest in a given field, their value was generally significantly higher than our value for the field, often 50% or more higher.

As the VP reflected on these findings, he made a strange (at the time) request. He asked me to calculate the split between the two companies, assuming that 1) each company knew better about the fields where only they had a working interest, and 2) the non-operating company knew better about the fields where only the other company had a working interest. In other words, he asked us to consider scenarios where 1) we were each right about our own fields and, conversely, 2) we were each wrong about our own fields. He was really challenging me to reconsider "owner's bias." I was skeptical that this would make a difference. And I was *wrong*. After completing the analysis, the difference in the split between the two methods was about 1%.

Our leaders said that that was a small enough difference for negotiations to lead to a deal. A couple of other team leaders and I were invited to accompany our senior leaders on a trip to the other company's HQ for final negotiations. I presented the findings of the "owner's bias" analysis to the leaders of both companies. After some discussion, we were asked to depart while the leaders talked and negotiated further. An hour or so later, the leaders emerged all smiles and shaking hands. The insurmountable difference had been resolved thanks to the unique approach guided by the challenge from my VP. **A deal was done.**

LEARNING POINT – When you reach an impasse in your analysis, take a step back and make sure "owner's bias" isn't skewing your perspective and clouding your vision. You will be amazed at how taking a different view can change your perspective and your outcome.

With the merger deal agreed, I was offered a coveted role for a mid-career technical professional. It was another planning role. I guess I didn't learn enough in my first go-round. The position was the upstream member of the corporate planning team in the Planning and Finance group, supporting the executive leadership Team and the CEO of Shell Oil Company. Talk about a major branch in my Career Tree. The tremendous opportunity came with great expectations for individual performance and growth. On to the next branch (and chapter) of my career.

+++++++++++++++++++++

In this chapter, you have seen the lessons I learned while starting my mid-career phase, including moving into supervisory roles, taking on special assignments, and branching out into assignments to broaden my understanding and perspective of the industry and expose me to senior levels of leadership. For those at this stage, you should start:

- Leveraging your technical skills and expertise to lead projects and make critical business decisions
- Having the confidence to rely on others to deliver their segments in support of common goals
- Considering short-term (1 or 2 year) assignments outside your core skill set to expand your capabilities and worth

- Expanding your personal skill set to lead others and be a representative for your organization in external interactions
- Becoming a mentor for junior staff to share your experience and learnings and help build their capabilities

REFLECTION QUESTIONS:

- Have I progressed my functional skills to a level where others seek my input and advice? If not, what more do I need to do?
- As I grow into mid-career roles, do I have mentor(s) (both personal and professional) to help me grow further? If not, who can I ask to help me consider where I can branch out and broaden my skill set and perspective?
- What other areas can I consider for "branching out" as a way of preparing for the future?
- Have I volunteered to be a mentor to someone else? If not, what is holding me back?

SUMMARY OF LEARNING POINTS – MID-CAREER BRANCHES

- As a supervisor, your success is dependent on the success of the individual team members. Knowing their strengths, areas of improvement, and building a sense of collective ownership is a foundation for success.
- REPEAT – Helping others improve and succeed isn't a sign of weakness. In fact, it is a sign of strength.
- REPEAT – When challenged and feeling overwhelmed, don't feel you have to do things by yourself. Seek out others for advice, guidance, and support. Working together, you can address the challenges at hand.

- Stopping a bad project is just as important as advancing a good project. Either way, you need to have a strong technical basis and thorough economic analysis for your recommendations. Let the work speak for itself.

- While building your core skills, two additional skills to work on are communication skills (both written and verbal) and financial knowledge. Being able to clearly and concisely communicate key points and demonstrate the profitability of your work will enhance your overall effectiveness.

- Just because you are the supervisor (or senior member of a team) doesn't mean you have all the answers. Learn to value and leverage the experience of your other team members.

- When facing a tough project (deadlines, challenging deliverables) spend the time to get alignment on expectations and final deliverables. Build on the varied skills and experience of the team members. Don't be afraid to bring different backgrounds together to solve a problem.

- When evaluating a portfolio of projects, remember that a high-level forecast is unlikely to be "accurate" at the individual component level. That said, there is confidence that the performance of the total portfolio can be reasonably predicted. The key is knowing at what level to trust the information.

- The move to a managerial role means growing new skills beyond your core functional skills. You have to become adept at effectively leading, coordinating, and interfacing with other teams to align and focus your teams on delivering results and working through others to get the results you want. You can no longer rely solely on your personal technical capabilities.

- Helping colleagues succeed doesn't have to be bad for you. As you help others build their skills, they will do the same. Collectively, the enhanced performance across all teams will give greater success than just one segment or team doing well.

- Team culture can't be demanded. Like trust, it has to be built on solid relationships and the belief that everyone is aligned on the shared objectives and will give their all for the team to succeed. Aligned goals and trust drive team success, not individual superstars.

- When you reach an impasse in your analysis, take a step back and make sure "owner's bias" isn't skewing your perspective and clouding your vision. You will be amazed at how taking a different view can change your perspective and your outcome.

Chapter 5

Supporting the Executive Leadership Team – Another Planning Branch

There will be times in your career when you may be offered a unique assignment that gives extraordinary opportunities for interacting with senior leaders. This chapter will explore my experience in one such role and how successful performance positioned me for an executive role. The new assignment was a major step up toward significant future positions. Learning opportunities would abound.

MORE PLANNING – BUT ON A HIGHER LEVEL

After successfully supporting the creation of the new regional partnership in West Texas, I was off to my new role as a corporate planner. The primary deliverable of the corporate planning team was compiling the annual and 5-year plan for Shell Oil with details from Upstream (Exploration & Production), Downstream (Refining & Marketing), and Chemicals. When the Onshore VP told me about the new role, he said it was a fantastic opportunity with lots of exposure to the top leadership of Shell Oil. But he also advised that "you can die from exposure." I think he was joking. He encouraged me to keep doing my best and take advantage of the opportunity.

The corporate planning team was comprised of four individuals. We were all mid-career (10 to 15 years' experience) representatives from each business segment, along with a financial representative. While we each had accountability for the completeness and quality of our individual sectors, we were judged based on the overall performance of the team. As mentioned in the previous chapter, the corporate planner role was a coveted job and was often seen as a stepping stone to the executive ranks. The challenge for me was to take full advantage of the opportunity by building my skills, perspectives, and network to position myself for future leadership roles.

We also got to work on special projects such as writing speeches for the CEO, evaluating potential M&A candidates, advising on sector collaboration opportunities, and working with senior leaders to define the Key Performance Indicators for their businesses.

One key opportunity in the corporate role was interacting with senior leaders across different sectors of the company. While each planner focused on their parent sector for the annual plan compilation, we served as the backup for a second sector. The opportunity to learn more was only as valuable as our willingness to be curious about an area that was not our specialty. When we leveraged the experience and expertise of others, we truly expanded our horizons and built our capabilities and industry knowledge.

LEARNING POINT – When given the chance to broaden your horizons, don't take things for granted. Be curious and put in the effort to truly learn from others. Doing so will broaden your perspective and enhance your overall skills, thereby increasing your value to the organization.

PERSONAL IMPACT

The compilation of the annual plan was time-consuming at certain times of the year, but it was not really mentally taxing. Most of us had held prior planning roles in our respective sectors. The time factor posed some personal challenges, as I had a young daughter at home and my wife was working as well. For family considerations, we downsized and moved from the suburbs of Houston to a neighborhood closer to downtown, cutting our respective commute times by more than half from over an hour to less than 30 minutes. While the change in distance was relatively small, the time gained had a tremendous positive impact on our collective mental health. As my wife said, I was a terrible commuter. This would start a trend in our family housing decisions for years to come.

LEARNING POINT – Often, taking on jobs with increased responsibilities also means increased demands on your time. It is critical to your personal life to find the right balance point between work, family, and friends. Value your time and use it wisely.

MAKING AN IMPACT BEYOND PLANNING

While the planning activities took up most of our time, the team members still had the chance to get involved in other projects within the larger group. In the second year of my assignment, I was called into my VP's office and informed that I needed to travel to Dallas the next day. There was a "super secret" assignment, and my experience in leading the technical assessment in the West Texas merger would be vital to the team.

The next morning, a few of us flew up to Dallas. We had our internal pre-meeting before the meeting with the other parties. We learned that two companies in California were planning to merge, like the West Texas deal. Now I understood why I was a part of the team. It was a chance to leverage my experience, share with others, and help streamline the process of reaching an agreement on the terms for the new combined company. It was wonderful to feel valued and see your efforts have a direct impact on project execution.

Over the next several months, we made multiple trips to DFW airport, meeting in one of the conference rooms in the adjacent hotel. There were four groups represented: corporate advisors from the two parent companies and leadership and technical representatives from the two operating companies in California. As we developed a common objective and approach, the wariness and fears slowly disappeared. After about three or four months, the process was made public, and the teams also started making visits to the fields in California. In the end, reaching an agreement on the value and relative split of the new organization was easier than my previous experience and was completed in about half the time. The project was a great success.

LEARNING POINT – When a project needs your skill set, step up and step in. Take a lead role and don't be shy.

LEARNING POINT – By building common objectives and agreeing on the process for completing work, you can quickly bring a team into alignment, which significantly helps in overcoming obstacles.

I NEED TO DO WHAT?

One of my most unusual (and valuable) experiences in the corporate planning role was when a colleague and I were tasked with writing a speech for our CEO to give as a keynote address at an industry conference. Our VP gave us a week to bring the draft speech to him for review and then share it with the CEO. To start, we each took a shot at drafting the speech individually. When we shared our drafts with each other, we wondered if we were given the same assignment. Mine was very technical and data-centered (as you would expect from a big nerd). My colleague's version was very conceptual and ethereal. We wondered how in the world we could complete the assignment.

In the past, I would have dug my heels in and said mine was the best. However, I had taken my Covey training to heart and believed in Habit #5 of Seek First to Understand, then to be Understood. Fortunately, my colleague shared the same belief. We wondered how we might combine the two. With that in mind, we each took a pass at combining the two versions. Interestingly, our combined versions were very similar and only required minor tweaking to come to an agreed final version. We reviewed it with our VP and anxiously waited for his feedback.

He said it was unique but also powerful in its message. The CEO liked the proposed speech and made a few minor changes but kept the tenor and central themes of the speech. After the conference, he said the speech had been well received by the audience. Later that year, the speech was chosen as one of the top keynote speeches in the industry. My colleague and I were pleasantly surprised and honored. For me, it showed the power of leveraging different perspectives and mindsets.

LEARNING POINT – Working with others who have different views, perspectives, and/or styles can be a challenge, but only if you let it. By leveraging each team member's views and working together, the outcome can be powerful and impactful. Let your differences drive greater value.

The normal rotation for the Corporate Planning assignment was generally one to two years. As my first year was concluding, the VP asked if I would like to stay for a second year. I had started working on some additional projects with more financial aspects than technical. I enjoyed working on projects that ranged from researching value drivers for oil and gas companies to evaluating key metrics for incentive compensation programs. I have jokingly said that over the 2+ years in the corporate planning role, I was able to get the equivalent of my "on-the-job" MBA.

The 2+ years as a Corporate Planner were a fantastic learning experience, but as the second year concluded, it was time to move on. The assignment had been challenging, enlightening, and in some ways exhausting. Luckily, I interviewed and was selected to be the new GM for Shell's oil and gas activities in

Michigan. So, after 15 years of building my trunk (critical core functional skills) and branching out through broadening assignments, field operations, and gaining a corporate-level perspective, it was time to put it to the test of leading an organization from the top. Funny thing, though, the learning didn't stop.

+++++++++++++++++++

This chapter focused on my experiences and learnings from a unique role supporting the corporate leadership team. For those who may find themselves in such a role, you should consider the following:

- Treat each assignment as a learning opportunity. You may be asked to undertake some tasks that don't make sense at the time of the assignment but can be eye-opening upon reflection.
- Pay attention to the rationale corporate leaders use in making key decisions. These insights will be of tremendous value if you move into similar roles.
- Do your best at each task assigned to you. While it is a job for you, the role is often an extended interview for future executive roles.
- Use the opportunity to expand your professional network, adding members from the executive support team.

REFLECTION QUESTIONS:

- What key insights did I gain from each project?
- What existing biases did I identify as I learned more about how the organization works?
- Did I do my best, no matter the task, or did I coast?

- Did I leverage my interactions with senior leaders to develop my own leadership style? What key attributes did I try to emulate?

SUMMARY OF LEARNING POINTS – SENIOR EXECUTIVE SUPPORT

- When given the chance to broaden your horizons, don't take things for granted. Be curious and put in the effort to truly learn from others. Doing so will broaden your perspective and enhance your overall skills, thereby increasing your value to the organization.
- Often, taking on jobs with increased responsibilities also means increased demands on your time. It is critical to your personal life to find the right balance point between work, family, and friends. Value your time and use it wisely.
- When a project needs your skill set, step up and step in. Take a lead role and don't be shy.
- By building common objectives and agreeing on the process for completing work, you can quickly bring a team into alignment, which significantly helps in overcoming obstacles.
- Working with others who have different views, perspectives, and/or styles can be a challenge, but only if you let it. By leveraging each team member's views and working together, the outcome can be powerful and impactful. Let your differences drive greater value.

Late Career

Growing in Stature and Bearing Fruit

Chapter 6

Moving into the Executive Ranks

After 15+ years of experience of planting the seed of my career in the oil and gas industry, growing my trunk with strong functional skills, and branching out with early leadership roles and special assignments, I was entering the late career stage with my move to the executive ranks. This was the time to grow in stature as a leader and start bearing fruit.

This chapter will explore the challenges and opportunities that come as you take on an executive role, with emphasis on defining vision, building culture, and leading a team to overall success.

STEPPING UP – FIRST-TIME EXECUTIVE

The Onshore US Division had recently refocused on geographic regions with an emphasis on improving the delivery of promised results on production and costs. My new role was the Asset/General Manager for Michigan, which brought along its share of challenges and opportunities. I immediately identified three challenges.

The first was geographic. My office was in Houston, along with the other GMs and the VP. The Michigan Asset team was split between two locations, with the technical staff in Houston and the operations teams spread across Michigan. This also meant that members of my leadership teams were in two different locations. My job was to effectively lead the split team as a single unit, even though we are separated by 1400 miles. As I started my role, I made a commitment to spend time in Michigan each month, with a personal target of being at the office and the field at least once a month. I would soon learn the value of frequent flyer miles.

LEARNING POINT – When stepping into a new leadership role, making a connection to your staff is critical. Being physically present whenever possible significantly accelerates the process of connecting and aligning with your team.

In some ways, the second challenge was more daunting. Two of the members of the leadership team I inherited were from my peer group at work. They had started a couple of years before I had, and I had now been promoted to be their boss. We had moved from being peers and colleagues to being boss and employees. My challenge was how to assume the position of authority without damaging past working relationships. Also, both leaders were good at their respective positions. I needed to count on them to deliver if the organization was going to succeed. Taking heed of a past learning point about not being a jerk as I moved into leadership roles, I knew I had to both establish myself as the leader and also tread carefully to get their buy-in and commitment. This is where the third challenge came into play.

For the past couple of years, the Michigan organization had done well but not great. The third challenge facing me in my new role was improving performance in production delivery, cost control, and safety performance. The performance of new wells that were to be drilled over the next few years was also included in these three areas. I was starting my GM role at the beginning of the calendar year, which was also the start of our planning year. The targets for the organization had already been set before I became the GM. But I was ultimately accountable for the organization's performance.

I used the third challenge to address all three potential areas of conflict. Shortly after starting the role, I assembled the key technical and operations staff, along with my leadership team, to discuss the year's targets. I also asked the two members of my peer group's leadership team to lead the discussions, since they had been part of the formulation of the business plan.

One of my early decisions was to hold this meeting in Michigan. I had quickly picked up on a potential divide between the two locations. I felt that the Houston members traveling to Michigan would be more effective at bringing the two groups closer together. We spent a few days together reviewing the targets while outlining challenges and key actions to ensure success. At the end of the session, the group was more aligned and energized than it had been in a while. We also committed to reviewing our performance as an accountable group in person at least once a quarter. We were off to a good start, but now we had to follow through on our talk and our commitments.

LEARNING POINT – When called upon to lead others who have recently been your peers, pressing your position of authority is not the most effective means of success. You need to leverage their experience and expertise and seek their input on critical decisions. Showing them respect helps ensure team dynamics are supportive rather than destructive.

LEARNING POINT – As you start a new leadership role, gaining alignment on critical deliverables for the organization, including focal points for accountability, potential threats, and areas requiring support, is critical in helping ensure early success.

IMPROVED PERFORMANCE

Over the course of that first year, I could see the team pulling together and our performance improving across the board, from operational safety, production efficiency, cost control, and overall volume and profitability. There was also more interaction between the technical teams in the two locations and between the technical and field operations teams. Things weren't perfect, but they were definitely improving. The teams were gaining confidence in their ability to meet and exceed our goals and targets. As my first year as GM was coming to a close, I was excited about what the new year would bring. I didn't know the challenges that would come my way.

PERSONAL TIME VS WORK TIME– FINDING THE RIGHT BALANCE

During that first year as GM, I had been traveling a fair amount, averaging 2 trips per month from Houston to Michigan. As mentioned previously, being present in the field and engaging teams in both locations was starting to bear fruit in our overall delivery of results. I thought the same was true for my home life. Boy, was I wrong, and it took an innocent comment from my 6-year-old daughter to hit home.

It was early November, and I was preparing for another trip to Michigan before the holidays and before the weather turned bad. Remember, I grew up in central Mississippi. Snow, when we got it, tended to shut all transportation down. As I was packing my suitcase, I overheard my wife ask our daughter what she wanted for Christmas. She replied that she would like a Barbie doll but said that she didn't need the Ken doll as dads were never home. **That was a dagger straight to my heart.** While I thought I had been doing a great job balancing the demands of leading teams in two different states with the demands of being a husband and father, this was direct feedback to the contrary.

I still made that trip, but I also informed my team that I would not be able to travel more than once a month going forward. Given that this was still the late 1990s, it meant more time on the telephone with my leadership team members in Michigan and slightly longer stays on my trips to the field. But in the end, my balance point shifted to spend more time in Houston and more time with family members while home, including lunches with my daughter at her school. In the end, my daughter's heartbreaking comment led me to genuinely reflect on what I wanted from my career and the types of roles I would consider in the future. What started as a stark comment on my availability to everyone led to a wonderful Christmas present for the whole family: more time together.

LEARNING POINT – As you grow in your career, you will be faced with choices of roles to undertake. In addition to career growth, consider the impact on your relationships, especially with your family. While each individual is different, reflect on finding the work-life balance point that is right for you.

MISSED OPPORTUNITIES

The business was running well, and my change in travel schedule to fewer trips to the field was helping me improve my Dad Score (see Calvin and Hobbes) at home. Overall, the Michigan Asset was delivering its production, safety, and financial targets, even in the face of lower commodity prices in 1998/1999. The organization had moved into the top tier of performance in the region across all measures. Many of our competitors in the area were struggling. We were creating competitive advantages in all areas of our business, from operational uptime and efficiency to capital costs of new wells and ultimate recovery from each well.

During the spring of 1999, I hosted the head of the US Upstream organization on a field visit. We visited several different field locations, including rigs drilling new wells, producing wells, and processing plants. While traveling from location to location, I discussed our competitive advantage and the struggles of some of our competitors. I noted several opportunities to expand our holdings and operations in the area. While interested, the leader was not ready to pursue any acquisitions. My leadership team and I were disappointed, but we didn't let this deter us from continuing our process improvement journey.

Over the next few months, we continued to exceed our targets. By mid-summer, we convinced the US Upstream leadership to make a bid for a distressed competitor. Our team was elated and worked to analyze the opportunity and prepare a competitive bid. When the bids were opened, we were number two and had been outbid by over 15 million dollars, or 7 to 8% of our bid. We were in the ballpark, but not close enough. Though disappointed in the outcome, the teams continued to deliver their top performance.

By the end of the summer, we learned two things that would have given us the winning bid. First, our corporate view on forward natural gas price increased. This change, if used in analysis, would have made our bid on par with the winner. Second, the winning company had a past strategy of finding price reductions during due diligence and applied that same approach to this bid, cutting its final price by over 5%. The combined effect is that we would have had the winning bid and significantly increased our holdings in the area. Alas, it was not to be.

LEARNING POINT – Outstanding performance can create opportunities for growth and expansion but doesn't guarantee a successful outcome. Either way, don't stop your focus on continuous improvement and delivering on commitments.

CHALLENGES ON LEADERSHIP STYLE

While traveling across Michigan during this same field visit with the head of the US onshore operations, I was granted the "opportunity" to discuss my leadership style and approach to running the business. I had always taken pride in interacting with the staff on my teams, engaging with the "why" behind actions, seeking input from others, and making informed decisions. The feedback from the big boss was that my approach could take too long to get results, and I should be more like him: forceful, direct, and even intimidating. I shared my views and said I respectfully disagreed. While yes, engaging with others could take longer to see a change in operational performance, my experience was that it led to longer and more sustained results versus an approach of force and threats, which gave a spike in performance that was rarely sustained for any length of time. I also emphasized the results that the team was delivering, which were amongst the best in the whole division, as proof of my approach. We left the conversation there, or so I thought.

As summer turned into fall, the organization started a redesign. The company was consolidating some leadership positions in Houston and adding a leadership role in New Orleans, which was offered to me, starting in January 2000. Since we had lived there previously, and our kids were in kindergarten and elementary school, my wife and I decided it was not that big of an issue, although it would mean she would be taking "early retirement" as her company did not have any offices in New Orleans, and remote work was not an option in 2000.

Along with the "request" to change roles, I was also given some further feedback on my performance as a leader. I was given high marks for the results versus targets for all the numerical metrics. However, it was noted that I had not been proactive in sharing the best practices and actions we had taken in the Michigan assets to achieve our outstanding results. The feedback was that while our team had done very well, our success was essentially limited to just our team. If I, and my leaders, had shared our processes and approach to business with the other assets in the portfolio, then it was likely they could have improved their performance as well.

I was in denial for a while and pushed back on the feedback. My thoughts and comments were that my primary role was to deliver outstanding performance from my assets and that I had done so. Then came the coaching moment. My VP sat me down and said that, as I moved into more senior roles, including the Michigan GM role, I also had a responsibility to help the broader organization do its best. This meant helping others do better, not just crushing it in my own assets. This was humbling to hear. I had forgotten one of the lessons from my first supervisor role. After taking some time and reflecting on the key message in the feedback, I committed to 1) becoming more open in seeking feedback on my performance from all levels (staff, peers, bosses) and 2) sharing with my colleagues what was happening in my business and how it might help them.

REPEAT LEARNING POINT – Helping others improve and succeed isn't a sign of weakness. In fact, it is a sign of strength.

LEARNING POINT – When given feedback on performance improvement, don't jump to denial, pushback, or become defensive. Take time to reflect on the key message being delivered and consider multilayered actions you can take to improve.

BACK TO THE GULF AND LEARNING TO HELP OTHERS

With my move back to New Orleans and my new role, I had a new boss, new colleagues on his leadership team, and my own leadership team. The role was the GM for the Mature Assets and covered the operations and engineering for the fields that spanned the shallow waters (< 600' water depth) of the Gulf of Mexico, along with a couple of deepwater fields that were past initial well development.

I was also in a unique position. I was now the GM for many of the fields I had been the engineer on some 15 years before. I'm not sure the current engineers on those projects were thrilled, but I found it very interesting to see the outcome of actions that I had a hand in designing.

During my first year in the Gulf role, our VP strongly pushed to improve our operations across all assets. Keeping in mind the feedback I had received in my prior role, I volunteered to use a couple of my assets as the testing ground, one shallow water fixed platform and one deepwater Tension Leg Platform (TLP). The project would require support from my leadership team, and specifically from the operations managers for the two fields in the trial, as their offshore teams would be heavily involved. A key to success was finding champions from the field staff to help educate and convert their coworkers. An interesting finding was that some of the best champions were not the leaders but early adopters who saw the value of the improvement actions.

LEARNING POINT – When driving change and/or continuous improvement activities, finding champions within the affected groups is critical to jump-start the adoption of the new process and drive the desired results.

After a few months, as the two fields started showing significant performance improvement, the other GMs on the leadership team were eager to get some of the action. Again, keeping in mind the previous feedback, I worked with the other leaders to create a process for sharing our learnings and for jump-starting improvement actions in their teams and fields. Learning to identify the right champions was critical to success. By forming a team of champions, we greatly accelerated the pace of improvement actions, and the Offshore division as a whole began exceeding our goals.

VALUE CREATION

As we implemented the actions from the pilot project across all the fields in the Mature Assets, operational performance started improving. This enhanced performance increased the profitability of the fields and opened up some opportunities for new production. However, most of the opportunities required capital investment. The company had a backlog of deepwater development projects that would each cost several billion dollars of investment to bring into production. This limited the investment dollars for the Mature Assets projects. This meant that the Mature Assets projects were usually bypassed for funding, which was a point of frustration for my teams, as they knew that the projects would add value if they could be funded and executed.

After a couple of years of limited investment, the decision was made to sell the shallow water fields in the Mature Assets. After selling the assets, the staff would be redeployed to other projects, and the sales proceeds would be used to help fund more deepwater projects. The Mature Assets team readily embraced the goal of maximizing asset value, with field teams working to ensure the recent production gains from the continuous improvement project were embedded in day-to-day performance. The technical teams captured all the investment opportunities they had sought to fund over the prior years and were unable to execute.

One key to a successful transaction is setting the minimum price you are willing to accept. A final value of the fields was agreed upon with the senior leaders, including some discounted value of the investment opportunities.

As the sales process progressed, one leading candidate was identified as a preferred purchaser. Six months after the initial internal discussion and engaging with possible buyers, the two companies agreed on a final price. The Mature Assets teams had done such a fantastic job of outlining the value of the assets that the final agreed price was more than 50% above the internally agreed minimum price. We were all elated.

LEARNING POINT – Value can be "created" by outstanding performance. Value is often "realized" by effectively communicating performance levels and identifying areas for further gains.

VALUE REALIZATION X2

Over the next several months, the buyer of the assets executed several projects identified in the data room but never funded internally. The activities led to increased production for the fields and the new owner. As a result, the stock market capitalization of the new owner increased significantly above the amount they paid for the fields. The senior leaders made some comments expressing disappointment that we had sold the properties for less than they were worth. We quickly reminded them that the value increase for the new owners came through their executing a significant portion of the capital projects we had identified but had left unfunded for several years. For us as the seller, we got more than we expected, as the buyer assigned some value to potential projects. The new buyer got even more value by actually executing the projects (along with some price help from increasing commodity prices).

LEARNING POINT – While identifying opportunities yields potential value, successfully executing the projects yields value realization.

SO, WHAT'S NEXT?

While I was leading the sales process for the shallow water assets, the company was undergoing a global reorganization, creating new organizations focused on the Americas (North and South America), Europe, the Middle East & Africa, and Southeast Asia. All leadership jobs were open with an effective date in May. And I was in the process of eliminating my own job by selling off 90% of the assets in my organization. Needless to say, I was nervous about my future role. I discussed the situation with my VP and asked if I could apply for other jobs. He said no, that my first job was to get the best value for fields being sold and that they would have a job for me when the sale was completed. It wasn't clear yet what that job would be. So, head down, I went back to the task at hand but not without a little bit of trepidation.

As the effective date of the new organization approached and the sales process moved toward negotiations on a final price, I asked again about my future role. My VP told me that the role they had designated was back in Houston, as the manager of planning, strategy, and economics on the regional support team for the Americas. I was underwhelmed (and maybe a little frustrated) at the offered assignment. I told him that I had already done two Planning jobs previously. I had spent 4+ years (over 25% of my career to that point) in similar roles, and my preference was for a different role. My VP told me that this was the only role still open and that was where I needed to be. As I continued arguing, he gave me some advice that changed my perspective. He told me not to focus on the aspects of the job that I had already done, but instead to concentrate on the aspects of the job that were new and were learning opportunities.

LEARNING POINT – When taking on a new assignment, think of it in two parts. First, what skills and experience can you bring to the job that can help you have a foundation for success? Second, use the new aspects of the role as a learning opportunity. This is a vital opportunity to grow your skill set and broaden your perspective.

++++++++++++++++++++

This chapter has focused on the transition from the mid-career to late-career phase and the corresponding transition from manager and technical advisor to first-time executive. For those who may find themselves starting an executive role, you should consider:

- Spending time early in the assignment to build connections with individual teams and members of your leadership team.

- Focusing on alignment across the organization on vision, values, and key deliverables.

- If leading others who are your peers, take care to make them feel valued by leveraging their respective areas of expertise and experience. Make them trusted advisors, not competitors.

- Receiving feedback (positive and negative) as a gift to help you continuously improve your own performance.

- Focusing your teams on delivering top performance to create value for the organization.

- When starting a new role, consider what you bring to the role from your past experience and what you can learn from the role to prepare for future roles.

REFLECTION QUESTIONS:

- What have I done to connect with members of my leadership team? What do I know about them personally? What drives them?

- Are our organization's vision, values, and critical success factors known across all teams? If so, are we aligned to deliver them? If not, what more can be done to improve the alignment?

- As I push for success, am I sharing with others to help them improve as well?

- Is my team's performance creating value for the company? If not, what more do we need to do?

- Am I using each new assignment to learn new skills and prepare for future roles?

SUMMARY OF LEARNING POINTS – EXECUTIVE ROLES

- When stepping into a new leadership role, making a connection with your staff is critical. Being physically present whenever possible significantly accelerates the process of connecting and aligning with your team.
- When called upon to lead others who have recently been your peers, pressing your position of authority is not the most effective means of success. You need to leverage their experience and expertise and seek their input on critical decisions. Showing them respect helps ensure team dynamics are supportive rather than destructive.
- As you start a new leadership role, gaining alignment on critical deliverables for the organization, including focal points for accountability, potential threats, and areas requiring support, is critical in helping ensure early success.
- As you grow in your career, you will be faced with choices of roles to undertake. In addition to career growth, consider the impact on your relationships, especially with your family. While each individual is different, reflect on finding the work-life balance point that is right for you.
- Outstanding performance can create opportunities for growth and expansion but doesn't guarantee a successful outcome. Either way, don't stop your focus on continuous improvement and delivering on commitments.
- REPEAT– Helping others improve and succeed isn't a sign of weakness. In fact, it is a sign of strength.
- When given feedback on performance improvement, don't jump to denial, pushback, or become defensive. Take time to reflect on the key message being delivered and consider multilayered actions you can take to improve.

- When driving change and/or continuous improvement activities, finding champions within the affected groups is critical to jump-start the adoption of the new process and drive the desired results.
- Value can be "created" by outstanding performance. Value is often "realized" by effectively communicating performance levels and identifying areas for further gains.
- While identifying opportunities yields potential value, successfully executing the projects yields value realization.
- When taking on a new assignment, think of it in two parts. First, what skills and experience can you bring to the job that can help you have a foundation for success? Second, use the new aspects of the role as a learning opportunity. This is a vital opportunity to grow your skill set and broaden your perspective.

Chapter 7

Lateral Moves – Growing a Branch and Adding Skills

After five years and two assignments as the general manager of diverse technical and operations teams running both onshore and offshore fields, the next move was back to a service role for the organization with a much smaller team. While I initially thought this move was a sidetrack to my career and maybe even a step back, it really provided some key personal learning opportunities. Even as you climb towards the top of your Career Tree, there are opportunities to broaden your perspective and learn new skills.

This chapter will explore the challenges and opportunities of a lateral move, with an emphasis on learning from each interaction, developing your personal skills, developing others, and preparing for future roles.

BACK TO PLANNING – THE THIRD TIME IS THE CHARM

As the sale process for the Mature Assets was completed, my family and I made the move back to Houston. We moved back to our old neighborhood, finding a house that was just a few blocks from where we had lived before. This was an important step in helping my wife and kids settle back into a routine because they were able to reconnect with friend groups.

For me, the new job required a quick start, as the move happened midyear, right when the planning process was kicking off. Luckily, the planning process had continued to improve since my role as the Planning Manager, and I had a great planning team with a fantastic leader and great staff. Plus, this was an area of strength from prior assignments that I could bring to the role. The challenge was that the breadth of the portfolio had expanded beyond onshore and offshore US to now include Canada and South America. While the planning team knew the process, they (and I) had to learn the history and characteristics of the new fields in the portfolio.

Over the next few months, the planning team did a great job compiling the short– and long-term forecasts for the entire portfolio. Little did we realize that work on the planning process would help us develop the region's strategy. In particular, the challenge was how to balance the region's financial limits, from capital demands to operating costs. The portfolio had three main segments:

- Onshore US with modest capital costs for each well, mid-range unit operating costs, and relatively fast field decline rate
- Offshore US (deepwater – remember, I helped sell the mature, shallow water assets) with very high capital development costs, very low unit operating costs once online, and modest field decline rate

- Canadian oil sands, which had very low capital development costs, very high unit operating costs, and a flat production profile.

The discussions with the senior leadership team for the region started with which area should be supported. After further discussion and comparison of the value created from each segment of the portfolio, the discussion shifted. Instead of focusing on one OR the other segments of the portfolio, the discussion shifted to be more inclusive, focusing on how much of each should be included in the forward plan. This breakthrough led to a strong alignment across the new organization and set the foundation for successful performance over the next few years.

LEARNING POINT – When evaluating amongst multiple options, sometimes the best questions to ask are not either/or but instead AND. Finding the right balance between choices is often better than focusing on a single option. Also consider alternatives in case the primary options are no longer viable. Developing contingency plans is a great way to build the skills of team members.

LEADING IN A TOUGH SITUATION

About a year into my regional support role, I was given a difficult, special assignment that no one wishes for. I was asked to lead an internal investigation into a fatality that had occurred on one of the platforms in the Gulf, where I had previously been the General Manager. This was one of the few shallow water fields we retained after exiting that segment of the industry.

This was a difficult time for the family of the deceased and the crew that had been onsite when the fatality occurred. I formed an investigation team, calling on members from across the organization who could help us identify root causes that contributed to the situation in which the incident occurred. None of us relished the role, but we all understood that identifying and communicating the areas of concern would help the organization prevent future incidents.

The investigation team visited the offshore field to get a better understanding of the incident and its contributing factors. We reviewed the planned work scope, along with the physical layout of the platform and work area. We also interviewed field staff, office staff, and leaders. After an in-depth review, several factors stood out, including shortcomings in

1. Work planning
2. Risk Assessment
3. STOP WORK authority
4. Perceived leadership objectives and priorities

When we shared our findings, there was initial resistance from the leadership of the field and the Offshore Division. For a few minutes, it felt like the investigation team was going to fall victim to "shoot the messenger." After taking time to discuss our findings in more detail, everyone agreed that there were gaps in the message on safety, and more could be done to fully embrace STOP WORK. In the end, a tough assignment and tough message were completed, and the results were accepted.

LEARNING POINT – As a leader at any level, you must repeatedly and always communicate clearly the uncompromising importance of safety. You must also be aware of the impact of your words. If you immediately shift from talking about safety to asking about schedule and targets, your comments on safety are undermined.

LEARNING POINT – When delivering a tough message, expect resistance. Be calm and present your case professionally and purposefully. Engaging with others without becoming overly emotional or loud will give you a better chance at gaining alignment.

LEARNING TO DEVELOP JUNIOR STAFF

One of the perks of the regional support team was having great staff. Many of the team's staff were on their own broadening assignments and were often top performers in their respective core disciplines. This meant I didn't really have to deal with performance issues. My role as the (General) Manager of the organization was to help develop these emerging leaders into the best versions of themselves and to prepare them for future leadership roles (in addition to their current jobs). In my 20 months in the role, I had the privilege of mentoring and coaching some great future leaders. I can't (and won't) say that I am perfect, but the assignment allowed me the chance to pass along the lessons from my career, many of which I have presented already in this book. I think this was a starting point for my own transition from a leader focused on himself and what's next to one focused on how to help others succeed. Maybe this was an inflection point in my Career Tree growth. On reflection, with the emphasis on strategic planning and developing others, I was approaching my own transition from mid- to late-career. This transition was a step in personal and professional maturity. I was starting to truly demonstrate the late-career characteristics of growing in stature and bearing fruit, particularly around developing future leaders.

I look back with pride at the leaders across the industry whom I helped shape through their own mid-careers, molding them into the successful leaders they would become.

LEARNING POINT – As you grow as a leader, a true measure of your success is the positive impact you have in developing and maturing future leaders. This demonstrates growing in stature and bearing fruit in your late career stage. In many ways, you can receive great joy from seeing an individual grow into an outstanding leader.

ABILITY OR ACCESSIBILITY?

During this time, supporting the Americas Regional Leadership Team, with the expanded range of countries and cultures in the new organization, the region increased its efforts in Diversity, Equity, and Inclusion. Having grown up in rural Mississippi in the 1960s and 1970s, I had observed racism firsthand. I had a growing interest and passion for helping others, and the new focus on Diversity, Equity, and Inclusion was a possible opportunity to help make a difference.

One of the employee networks that was started was the Women's network. With a wife who had worked in the corporate world and faced challenges to lead operations teams and a young daughter who would someday enter the workforce, I was fully supportive of these efforts. I asked the regional leadership and the Women's network leadership if I could be an ally for their network. I was pleased and excited when both said yes.

One of the early meetings of the network leadership was a strategy planning meeting. Given my new role as an ally and my experience in planning and strategy, I was asked to join the workshop. I arrived that morning to find myself and an HR rep as the only 2 males in the room along with 15 women.

Little did I know that the event would be an eye-opening AHA moment in my life. We started the day with an icebreaker exercise. The facilitator asked us to stand shoulder to shoulder in a line they had taped across the middle of the conference room. We were then asked a series of 'societal norms' questions. Some of the questions that were asked included:

- If you are male, take a step forward; if female, stay put.
- If you are right-handed, take a step forward. If left-handed, take a step back.
- If you are married, take a step forward; if single, stay put; if divorced, take a step back; if married more than twice, take 2 steps back.
- If you grew up with both parents at home, take a step forward; if only one parent, take a step back.
- If you have a college degree, take a step forward; if you have an advanced degree, take 2 steps forward; if you only graduated high school, stay put; if you do not have a HS diploma, take a step back.
- If you were the first generation in your family to graduate from college, take a step back.

After a few questions, I was getting a little nervous. The men seemed to be the only ones consistently moving forward. As I remember, there were only one or two questions where I stayed in place or moved back. On all the others, I had stepped forward. When all the questions had been asked, I was the furthest forward from the starting point. Many of the women were clustered slightly forward of the center line, with a few even behind the starting point. I knew many of the women in the room and considered them to be very successful. What was going on?

Our facilitator asked several of us what we felt. My response was "Confused and a little embarrassed." When the facilitator asked me to expand further, I shared that I had grown up in poor/lower-middle-class rural Mississippi and that our state was not known for its outstanding academic record. I had self-funded my college education (through loans, scholarships, and work), studied hard, graduated Summa Cum Laude, landed a great job, and had worked hard demonstrating focus, diligence, tenacity, and productivity. I felt that I had "earned" my promotions and early executive position.

Thankfully, the facilitators didn't laugh at me. The facilitators thanked me for my honesty in sharing my experience and perspective. They acknowledged my hard work and success. But they also pointed out that for many of the questions that were asked of the group, I had met the societal norms for success, which had given me more frequent and greater access to opportunities to demonstrate my skills. The question before the workshop participants was, "What could we do as an organization (and individual leader) to ensure that everyone has equal access to opportunities to demonstrate their abilities?" What an individual then chose to do with that access was up to them.

At the end of the workshop, I was humbled, enlightened, grateful, and excited about what I could do to make a difference. What a powerful life lesson.

LEARNING POINT – As senior leaders, we need to work hard to ensure that our systems and processes are set up to give equal access to opportunities for every individual to demonstrate their skills and abilities. That is true Diversity, Equity, and Inclusion. The choice of how to respond to the opportunity is up to the individual. With equal access comes equal chance to grow, shine, and progress.

LEVERAGING YOUR CORE SKILLS

My new organization had a small team with a unique corporate responsibility: reporting the region's hydrocarbon reserves to the Securities and Exchange Commission. This is a legal requirement for any oil and gas company publicly traded in the US. The US-based portfolio had been fulfilling this duty for decades. Since reservoir engineering was my core discipline, I enjoyed engaging with this group and reviewing our submittal. As the group leader, I ultimately had to sign off on it. In some ways, it felt like I was an early-career engineer again, tapping into my technical side. While not required, I also felt that the responsibility for the group and my signature was also leveraging my PE license. With both my technical background and my professional certification, I was uniquely positioned to oversee this critical task.

During my second year in the regional support role, a critical issue affecting the global community was raised. The corporate headquarters had received a notification from the SEC regarding concerns about our reserve reporting from around the world. Several areas of the portfolio were identified for discrepancies in reporting versus our partners in the same fields. After an in-depth review, the global company was fined by the SEC. The only clean area in the external review was the Americas Region, with no findings. On reflecting on the findings from the other regions, it became clear that a lack of knowledge of the reporting requirements and spotty technical review and assurance had led to many of the issues cited by the SEC.

I was pleased with the performance of the Americas Region technical teams and my assurance/reporting team. At the same time, I was disappointed about the outcome for the rest of the company. It was a blemish on the reputation of a company for which I had felt immense pride for over 20 years. Little did I know that this global shortfall would lead to the next level of my Career Tree.

LEARNING POINT – Always make sure you know the requirements of a task, especially if you are a representative for the company. A lack of understanding/knowledge of the requirements (legal, contractual) can put you and the company in a position of legal peril.

MOVING ABROAD – STEPPING UP TO THE NEXT LEVEL

The regional support teams had been wrapping up our second year of the Regional Business Plan while the global reserves issue was being resolved. As the year was coming to an end, the RS teams were growing in capability and confidence. Our understanding of the portfolio, with the strengths and weaknesses of each segment, was helping position the Americas Region as a valuable part of the global portfolio.

As we moved into December, the new global CEO visited Houston and toured many of the offices. I was a part of the entourage accompanying him to the research labs. As a part of the walk around, I had a few minutes alone with the CEO. He asked me about my background, areas where I had worked, and the ongoing work in the regional support team. When I got back to my office later that afternoon, something seemed off. My boss was waiting outside my office. My heart was immediately in my throat, and I wondered what I might have done wrong.

I totally misread the situation.

"What do you think about moving overseas?" my boss asked.

"Well, my family and I considered it prior to the regional support role, but I was unsuccessful in landing that job. What would the new role be? And where?" I replied.

"You would be promoted to a Senior Executive as the Technical Director of Brunei Shell Petroleum (BSP) in the country of Brunei Darussalam on Borneo Island in Southeast Asia."

I was shocked. After capturing my breath, I said, "I need to do a little bit of research on the job, the area, and speak to my wife to gain her support before accepting, of course."

Needless to say, the rest of my afternoon was blown as my mind was going in a thousand directions trying to comprehend what the opportunity meant. I talked a bit more with my boss to learn what he knew about the new role and working in SE Asia.

He shared insights into the challenges facing the country and the company in Brunei. One of the areas of concern in the global reserves issue had occurred there. He also highlighted the traits I had that he thought would be of value. The role sounded interesting, but it would be over 12,000 miles away (and a 13-hour time difference) from friends and family in the US. I was excited and interested, but now came the most important step: getting my wife's support.

I met my wife at church for the mid-week dinner and activities. After all the events of the day, I wasn't really hungry. We got our kids settled into their activities, and I told my wife we needed to talk. I asked her to follow me to the church library. Once there, I got down a globe we had donated earlier that year. I spun it around and pointed to Borneo Island and the small dot of the country of Brunei Darussalam. I said that I (we) had been offered a role based there. I would need to be there by the end of March next year. She was shocked since we had only been back in Houston for less than 2 years. Later that evening, after putting the kids to bed, we did some more research about the country, the company, and the role. After praying, we decided that taking the proposed role would be a great opportunity for our entire family. I am thankful that I had a life partner who was willing to join me on this new adventure, even if it meant disrupting her life and connections.

PERSONAL LEARNING POINT – One of the most important decisions in your life is the choice of your life partner. Who you surround yourself with shapes how you approach life. For me, I have been blessed to find someone who is caring, loving, supportive, and willing to join me in adventures around the world.

Looking back, I had to admit that my VP's advice in New Orleans was correct. Taking on the regional support role and building my skill set opened opportunities for advancement and international assignments that would not have been possible if I had chosen my preferred role of continued operations. We had been truly blessed. LOOK OUT WORLD (AND BRUNEI), HERE WE COME.

REPEAT LEARNING POINT – When taking on a new assignment, think of it in two parts. First, what skills and experience can you bring to the job that can help you have a foundation for success? Second, use the new aspects of the role as a learning opportunity. This is a vital opportunity to expand your skill set and broaden your perspective.

LEARNING POINT – Even as an executive, broadening your skill set and building on your core skills will position you for roles of greater responsibility and accountability. Be ready to step into those roles.

+++++++++++++++++++

This chapter has focused on the lateral move to a service role, another broadening assignment in the midst of growing in stature as an executive. What I thought was a sidetrack turned into a launching pad for more senior roles. For anyone finding themselves in such a situation, you should consider:

- Finding the parts of the role where you can excel to demonstrate your value.
- Focusing on segments of the role where you can grow new skills and/or broaden your perspective.

- Reflecting on the opportunities you had to clearly demonstrate your capabilities.
- Taking time to develop others, serving as a mentor or advisor

REFLECTION QUESTIONS:

- Where have I excelled before, and how can I use those skills in my new role?
- What new learning opportunities does this role offer? Am I taking advantage of those opportunities? If not, why not?
- Am I using this lateral move to position myself to spring forward? Or fall back?
- Am I taking the time to develop others' leadership capabilities? If not, what is stopping me from offering my services as a mentor for someone else?

SUMMARY OF LEARNING POINTS – MOVING LATERALLY

- When evaluating amongst multiple options, sometimes the best questions to ask are not either/or but instead AND. Finding the right balance between choices is often better than focusing on a single option. Also consider alternatives in case the primary options are no longer viable. Developing contingency plans is a great way to build the skills of team members.
- As a leader at any level, you must repeatedly and always communicate clearly the uncompromising importance of safety. You must also be aware of the impact of your words. If you immediately shift from talking about safety to asking about schedule and targets, your comments on safety are undermined.

- When delivering a tough message, expect resistance. Be calm and present your case professionally and purposefully. Engaging with others without becoming overly emotional or loud will give you a better chance at gaining alignment.

- As you grow as a leader, a true measure of your success is the positive impact you have in developing and maturing future leaders. This demonstrates growing in stature and bearing fruit in your late career stage. In many ways, you can receive great joy from seeing an individual grow into an outstanding leader.

- As senior leaders, we need to work hard to ensure that our systems and processes are set up to give equal access to opportunities for every individual to demonstrate their skills and abilities. That is true Diversity, Equity, and Inclusion. The choice of how to respond to the opportunity is up to the individual. With equal access comes equal chance to grow, shine, and progress.

- Always make sure you know the requirements of a task, especially if you are a representative for the company. A lack of understanding/knowledge of the requirements (legal, contractual) can put you and the company in a position of legal peril.

- PERSONAL – One of the most important decisions in your life is the choice of your life partner. Who you surround yourself with shapes how you approach life. For me, I have been blessed to find someone who is caring, loving, supportive, and willing to join me in adventures around the world.

- REPEAT – When taking on a new assignment, think of it in two parts. First, what skills and experience can you bring to the job that can help you have a foundation for success?

Second, use the new aspects of the role as a learning opportunity. This is a vital opportunity to expand your skill set and broaden your perspective.

- Even as an executive, broadening your skill set and building on your core skills will position you for roles of greater responsibility and accountability. Be ready to step into those roles.

Chapter 8

Going Global – Climbing Higher in My Career Tree

My opportunity to become a senior executive in the company had arrived with my appointment as the Technical Director for Brunei Darussalam, 22 years after planting the seed of my career and seven years after moving into the late career phase. Given the importance of the role, the diverse cultures in the company, and the business performance challenges facing the organization, this was truly an opportunity in climbing my Career Tree to grow in stature and bear fruit.

This chapter will explore the challenges and opportunities that come with taking on a senior executive role, with emphasis on visioning for the future, guiding an organization to success, and leveraging the skills of the entire organization to turn performance around and have a positive impact.

NEXT STOP – OTHER SIDE OF THE WORLD

Having accepted the new overseas position, the next few months were a whirlwind. Time was spent engaging with my Houston team to ensure a smooth transition for my replacement. Then, time spent talking to my new boss in Brunei (either in early morning or late evening due to the time difference), discussing the scope of the role and key focus areas. Finally, there were cultural awareness classes for both my spouse and me to learn more about the country and how best to assimilate into the new country. Of particular focus were customs and expectations of being a non-Muslim in a Muslim country.

As the end of the first quarter of 2005 came to a close, everything was in place for me to head over. I gave a hug to my family and boarded the flight to Los Angeles and then Singapore before the connection to Brunei. My family was staying back in Houston until the end of the summer to finish school, close out the house, make final visits to our families, and then prepare to join me.

GETTING SETTLED

When I got to Brunei, I was excited for the possibilities of the new role. I was also exhausted. I was met at the airport by my executive assistant, Linda, and my driver, Jack. (I knew to expect that I would have an EA, but I never anticipated that I would need a driver. That would take some getting used to.) I also noticed that a late March day in Brunei felt like a typical summer day in Houston and New Orleans, hot and humid.

Over the next few years, I would learn that Brunei really had two seasons, "wet" and "dry." In the "wet" season, it rained 2 or 3 times per day. The "dry" season was much better as it only rained once per day. And all the days were hot and humid. One of my purchases after my first month in the country was several dehumidifiers. They were an absolute necessity. Without them, anything leather would start to mold, and your clothes would always feel damp and smell of mildew. Trust me, not a pretty sight or pleasant smell.

Although I was married, since my wife and family were not immediately joining me in the country, I was deemed an unaccompanied "single" male. As such, I was given temporary housing in the company "camp." My EA was a fantastic resource in understanding the transition to the new country and customs. With my position as Technical Director, I was one of the most senior expats in the company and country. Normally, I would be expected to have a live-in "amah" (domestic help). However, since I was a "single" male, it was against the law for me to have a female living in my house who was not my wife. It didn't matter much to me as I knew how to cook, clean, and do laundry. I started to protest that I could fend for myself, but my EA was very concerned and made sure that I got on a rotation for "help" with the house while I was at the office.

LEARNING POINT – If you find yourself in an area (or country) with different customs, don't just "trust your instincts." Be willing to take guidance from those more knowledgeable.

In the first few weeks, I spent part of my time learning the layout of the camp and nearby towns. I learned that I was allowed to drive myself to the office and on the weekends, but otherwise, Jack was my man. He showed me the various parts of the camp and the offices of some of my teams that were not housed in the headquarters. He also showed me the locations of key businesses (grocery store, restaurants, and other stores – no Walmart or Target). With time on my hands in the evenings and weekends, I also checked out the employees' club. We had our own golf course, swimming pools, tennis courts, sailing club, and library. Stepping out of my comfort zone, I took up sailing lessons and earned my pilot's license for catamarans. I also bought a set of golf clubs. I had played in the past but not recently. I soon found my weekends and many evenings full with sports activities. It was fun, and I was getting in better shape.

One of the biggest challenges of settling in was forming new friendships. I arrived in the country knowing no one else in the company or country. Also, almost half the expats technically worked in my organization, so I was either their boss, or their boss's boss, or even their boss's boss's boss. How do you form friendships when, ultimately, you lead the organization? Luckily, some of the expats who worked on other teams connected with me and gave me advice, particularly as this was my first expat experience, and they were seasoned veterans.

LEARNING POINT – Being a senior leader doesn't mean you have to isolate yourself. At the same time, it doesn't mean that you are best friends with all your staff. Finding the balance between leader and friend can be challenging. Learning to segregate the two aspects of your life, and being humble in both, makes each role easier.

BUSINESS FOCUS

Between the time I accepted the Technical Director (TD) role in December and arriving in Brunei in March, the Managing Director (MD) for the company (my boss) changed. I was on a final vacation with my family when I got a call from the MD who had given final approval for my move, saying that he was leaving Shell and that another senior leader would be the new MD. While I didn't know either person, I had never spoken to the new MD before my arrival. In fact, he arrived in the country only a few weeks before I did.

Irrespective of the change in the top position, I was given some clear instructions on my areas of focus for my role and the company executive leadership team. The overall performance of the company had been declining over the past couple of years, and the company had been one of the areas identified for problems in the global reserve issue the prior year. My charge was to help turn performance around by improving safety, volumes, and cost performance. As the Technical Director, I was also expected to bring an emphasis on technical rigor across all the teams and help grow the future field developments to support more production volumes. My initial engagements with my new MD reinforced the areas of focus.

I also learned more about the scope of my role. In addition to the MD, the Senior Leadership Team had a Finance Director overseeing all financial elements of the company, an HR Director overseeing all people policies and practices, including housing and the company school, and a Production Director overseeing the field operations and supporting technical teams. Everything left fell to the TD, namely me. That included exploration, early field development, well drilling and completions, geomatics, geophysics, logistics (air – helicopters; land – vehicles and equipment; and sea – marine vessels), construction, and, lastly, IT. *Wow*. An exciting scope and definitely an opportunity to broaden my skills, as I was in no way an expert in most of these areas.

LEARNING POINT – As you take on more senior executive roles, you will find yourself accountable for areas of the business where you don't have expertise. It is critical to leverage the experience and expertise of other leaders on your team. Your job is to put in place the policies, practices, and support systems to help your team succeed.

CULTURE COUNTS AND STYLE MATTERS

In accepting the role, I became one of the younger members of the senior executives across the globe. In my past behavior/leadership assessments, the traits of analytical/technical focus and being a driver for results were identified as dominant characteristics. I was certain that with these traits, I was well-positioned to quickly make the changes to get the company back on the right track. Little did I know that my moment of enlightenment on how to work in a different culture was coming.

In the office, I spent the first two to three weeks talking to different teams about what they did, who they interacted with, and getting their input on pain points and areas where they and the organization could improve. I also gathered information on where they needed additional support to succeed. As I reflected on my observations and findings from the first few weeks, I had a few ideas for improving the organization's technical support. In particular, I thought the technical teams within the asset teams were stretched thin between optimizing the performance of existing fields, drilling new wells in those fields, and maturing new extensions and fields in their geographic area of responsibility. I thought that creating a new team to advance new development opportunities nationwide would provide greater focus on future delivery while allowing the Asset teams to focus on activities to improve existing performance.

I was eager to make the changes and push forward with delivering improved performance. Taking in mind some of my past learning points, I shared my findings with my Production Director colleague. He was a Bruneian and was well respected in the company and with the government agencies. When we reviewed the pain points in the organization and my proposed changes, he thought they had merit. He also advised caution. In particular, he shared where past people in my role had run into challenges. One of the major pitfalls had been trying to push through changes without sufficient engagement with the affected parties, both within the company and with the government groups. I welcomed his input and advice and agreed to wait a few months before implementing my proposed changes.

I spent the next several months working within the existing organizational structure, confirming pain points and testing the potential impact of my proposed changes on projects and performance. I also had a couple of engagements with members of the regulatory agency in the government, who would have to approve any of my proposed changes. After six months of leading the organization, observing interactions among technical teams, and evaluating the potential impact of my proposed organizational changes, I sought an opportunity to present the new organizational model to the government agency overseeing the oil and gas Industry.

As it turned out, the meeting would take place during the period of Ramadan. This was my first Ramadan, and I was learning the ins and outs of the Islamic holy month. From my Bruneian EA, key Bruneian staff, and my Bruneian colleagues on the executive team, I learned about the fasting during the day and breaking the fast with family and friends after sunset each day. I also noticed changes in the normal routine in the office. The canteen was closed during the month. And the "tea ladies" no longer made their normal morning and afternoon rounds through the buildings. Instead, the large central atrium/auditorium was closed off, and all non-Muslim employees would come to that central location to get their tea and coffee. There was no public eating or drinking during this period.

[The "tea ladies" were a blessing. Each morning at 9 and in the afternoon at 2, they pushed their carts through the offices and offered employees hot tea, coffee, or Milo. I came to anticipate their arrival and enjoy their service. And if I asked nicely, they would even slip me an extra cup in between their rounds.]

For the meeting with the government agency, I brought a couple of my leaders with me. We were meeting with the agency's Deputy Director and some of his team. I presented our case for action and the proposed changes, what it would mean for organizational design, and the potential for improved performance in the appraisal and development of new fields and wells. After the presentation, we addressed questions and concerns from the government staff. One of their staff asked a question. In my response, I said, "I don't mean to put words in your mouth, but…" Before I could finish my comments, he had an immediate outburst – "This is the Holy Month. I put NOTHING in my mouth during the day." I was shocked and dumbfounded. I didn't know how to respond. After a moment of silence, I apologized for my comments. What I had thought was an "innocent" comment that is used all over the US, where I had spent the first 22 years of my career, was in fact a blunder. In my mind, I thought this might be a quick end to my assignment.

LEARNING POINT – A lack of knowledge of national culture can lead to missteps. Be aware and be knowledgeable about cultural norms. You may very well avoid embarrassment from putting your foot in your mouth.

After the heated response to my comment, the temperature in the room chilled considerably. The government team thanked us for the input but told us that we were rushing the change and needed to take more time before making the proposed changes. There was nothing more I could say or do. I kept my mouth shut (I had already put my foot in it just a few moments earlier) and got in my car for my driver to take me back to the office.

I was *frustrated*. Rushing the change? I had waited over five months before bringing my proposal forward for their review and approval. The "driver" personality in me was struggling to figure out a way forward. Over the next week, I reflected on the meeting and the comments made. I sought the counsel of my Bruneian colleague on how to move forward. He listened and then gave me some good advice. He said that while he liked my drive to push forward with solutions, the Bruneian culture was one based on relationships and hierarchy. He said not to lose hope and that rarely (if ever) did a proposed change or project get approved by the government on the first try, even by him, a Bruneian himself. His words were, "David, you have a great proposal, and it is going to add value to the company. But your approach is not going to work. You cannot force the government to approve the proposed change."

Instead, his advice was not to give up but instead to focus on frequent engagements with the government leaders. I needed to listen to their concerns about my proposed changes and take their comments into consideration by involving their team in the organization design and staffing changes. He also said making some tweaks in the proposal based on their input would give them a sense of ownership in the outcome. Bottom line, I need to change my style because the government was not. I could either continue to be **frustrated** or become **productive.**

I appreciated his candor and perspective. After further reflection, I took the steps he had proposed. I met with the government team several times each month to review our company's performance in the areas of the proposed changes, gather their input, and work toward a common solution. By the end of my first year in the country, the government had approved the revised organizational design. We were on our way to making the changes and recruiting staff to fill the new positions. In hindsight, the revisions did not significantly alter the desired outcome or impact and were a better fit for the Bruneian culture. I learned that style and approach matter, and listening to and involving others in important decisions is better.

LEARNING POINT – National culture trumps personal style. Be prepared to change your approach or accept frustration and delays. You may find that the change in approach alters your leadership style for years to come. Your adaptability will also be a role model for other leaders in your organization, helping them navigate their own development.

GRIEVING FROM AFAR

While my work on the organizational design was underway, the summer was coming to an end, and it was time for my family to join me in Brunei. After participating in the celebratory events for the Sultan's birthday in mid-July, I returned to the US to help finish with the last details of the move, visit friends and family across the US, and travel with my wife and kids back to Brunei.

In early August, we made the trip to Mississippi to visit both sets of parents (and grandparents), as we would not be back in the US until the following July. On our way back to Houston, we stopped in New Orleans to see friends from our time there just a couple of years before. We happened to be there during a block party. We spent the day catching up and sharing about our upcoming move. We had a great time, great food, and great reconnections. We said our goodbyes and headed back to Houston to do our last shopping, pack our essentials shipment and large suitcases. After some final fun activities in and around Houston, with a little trepidation, nerves, anxiety, and curiosity, we boarded our flight to Brunei, via LA and Singapore.

We arrived some 30+ hours later and were met by my driver and EA. They greeted my family as if they had known them for years. The kids couldn't believe we had a driver. It was late August. At least one thing was familiar: the heat and humidity. After we cleared customs, our driver took us to our new home in the jungle. Our "amah" met us at the house and greeted us all with a hug. (It was now legal for her to be in the house, since my family was in the country.) We were all exhausted but also excited to finally be in our new home. We had some snacks and lemonade on the screened-in back patio. The kids decided to check out the yard and walk to the edge of the surrounding jungle. As they did, a group of monkeys came out. The kids thought they were cute until the monkeys started chasing them back to the house. They made it back safely but learned a valuable lesson about being wary of the wildlife.

We spent the weekend getting settled, driving around the camp and surrounding towns, visiting the school, and, more importantly, the club. They loved the pool and beach. As the new week started, I returned to work after having been away for several weeks. My wife was busy getting our new house set up, and the kids were making new friends.

We all woke up on Tuesday morning, August 30th, to the disaster that had struck New Orleans, Hurricane Katrina. The neighborhood block party we had attended 3 weeks before was now under 10 feet of water. We didn't know if our friends were safe, and if they were, where they had evacuated. And we had no way to get in touch with them. Our anxiety level, which was already high, suddenly exploded. All we could do was pray for their safety. We couldn't go back since we didn't know where anybody was located, and the city of New Orleans was shut down and flooded. The worry wasn't helping with getting settled, but we had to move forward. All we could do was grieve from afar.

[After we moved back to the US and ultimately back to New Orleans, we learned that because we had not lived through and experienced the tragedy of Katrina personally, there would always be a level of separation between us and our friends and neighbors who had.]

REPEAT LEARNING POINT – Life can change suddenly. Pursue the things you love, both in your work and your life.

THE VALUE OF DIVERSITY IN LIFE

After recovering from the shock of Hurricane Katrina back in the US, our family started getting settled in our new home in Brunei. The kids were preparing for the start of school, and my wife was exploring the community and the various activities at the club. My EA and driver were a great help. I knew it, but the rest of the family soon learned that we were one of only a small handful of American families in the country. There were a fair number of Dutch and British (home countries of the company), Australians, New Zealanders, Malaysians, and Indonesians (relatively close proximity to Brunei), Nigerians, and Venezuelans (larger global operations for the company). At first, this realization that we were a minority nationality in the country was a shock, and for my wife and daughter, a cause of initial concern.

As I talked with my wife, I explained that most of the activities around the camp were run by employees and their spouses. I encouraged her to look for an area where she could have a positive impact and feel comfortable. She quickly discovered the camp library and learned that the past "librarian" had recently departed, since her husband had taken another posting. As an avid reader, this was an exciting opportunity. She stepped into the role and never looked back. Through her work at the library, she met other spouses and built a network of friends. The connections also led her to a newly discovered passion, quilting. Over the years we spent in the country, she embraced living abroad, explored the region, picked up new hobbies, and made lifelong friends.

Our son was entering the third grade when we moved. His 2nd-grade class in Houston had 5 or 6 classes and over 100 students. Almost everyone in that grade was American, and a great majority had been born and raised in Houston. When he went to class at the company school, there were only 2 sections and 32 students. The amazing fact was that over 20 countries were represented. As his parents, we thought that was amazing. He thought nothing of it. It just meant that many of his friends spoke other languages. His birthday was 5 or 6 weeks after we arrived in the country. We rented a water slide, ordered pizzas from the local pizzeria (sorry, no Domino's or Pizza Hut), and invited all of his classmates (and their parents). It was great to see all the kids running around, having fun, without a single care that someone else was from a different country or had a different accent. Kids were just kids, no matter their country of origin, and we were living away from our home country. He also learned how to play cricket, rugby, and golf. While his golf skills were useful in making the Varsity golf team when we got back to the US, the other two sports were fun but not very useful back in the US. It seems that a cricket batting stance doesn't really translate to baseball. Who knew?

Our daughter had the most challenges in transitioning to the new situation. She had just turned 13 in the months before we moved. She was also one of the smaller students in her class back in the US and was relatively shy. She was entering the 8th grade, which meant that she would be attending the International High School. The school was located in the capital, Bandar, about 60 miles away. This would mean an hour+ commute each way each day. She would have a driver to take her back and forth. Her school days would start with a 6 a.m. pickup to make sure she was not tardy for the 7:30 start of classes.

We visited the campus a couple of days before school started to get her class schedule and her uniform, a skirt down to her ankles, and a blouse and tie. That was quite a change from the US. At least there wouldn't be a debate about what to wear each day. On the first day of class, I got her up at 5 a.m., and she was dressed before her pickup time. However, at that moment, the nerves kicked in, and she didn't want to go. I knew I couldn't let her miss, as it would do nothing to improve her confidence. As much as I hated to do it, I got her out the front door, closed it, and said that she couldn't come back in until she got back from school. She was upset and reluctantly got into the car with her driver. With no way to check in with her during the day, my wife and I were a little worried about how she would do. When she got home that afternoon, she quickly changed and went to the club to meet some of the other girls from her year in school. I think that helped with her transition. There was still a bit of anxiousness in the first couple of weeks, but each day got easier. Like her brother, she started enjoying all the different friends she was making. They started joking about the various words from the US, UK, Australia, and New Zealand for the same object. As the months went by, I saw her come out of her shell, growing more confident and surer of herself.

We each handled our transition to our new community differently. We all realized that the variety of people we interacted with in our work, schools, and activities brought a richness of experience we couldn't get elsewhere. We each had to grow personally, but the end result was well worth it. Over the years of our assignment, families came and went. As a family, we learned to make fast friends and say quick goodbyes. Overall, each of us felt that our time abroad was a fantastic life experience that we would not have changed.

LEARNING POINT – When faced with a new and unfamiliar environment, you can retreat into your shell and close off others, or you can take the (tough) step to put yourself out there, engaging with others, and build new relationships (and even friendships).

NEVER BLOCK A SNEEZE

This next lesson is personal, but it is valuable to everyone.

We were all settling into our daily routine after a couple of months in the country. For me, I would wake up at 5 a.m. to get our daughter up and ready for school. While she was getting ready, I would prepare some breakfast, do my daily meditation, and review my calendar of events for the day. On one particular morning, as I went into my daughter's room, I felt a sneeze. Not wanting to startle my daughter and our dog, who was sleeping in her room, and then wake up everyone, I covered my nose and held the sneeze in. BIG MISTAKE. As I stifled the sneeze, I felt a popping in my right ear. I didn't think anything about it and went about the rest of my morning routine.

As I was getting dressed for the office, I noticed that I felt some pressure in my ear similar to when you take off in an airplane. I did the standard response of trying to yawn really big and holding my nose and swallowing, but it didn't seem to clear up.

140

I went into the office and started my workday. My EA came in to review the day's schedule. It sounded like she was talking in a tunnel. I asked her to reschedule my morning meetings, and I went to see the company doctor. I explained the events of the morning. He examined my ear and told me I had burst my eardrum. *Man, what a sneeze!* That would have been bad enough but could have been overcome. Then he took a tuning fork, struck it on the table, and held it to my forehead. I could hear the ringing in my right ear. Uh oh, I thought. The doctor said it out loud. That couldn't be good. It seems that in addition to blowing out my eardrum, I had also shifted the bones in my ear and compressed my ear canal. No wonder I couldn't clear the pressure that I felt in my ear. After that, the doctor conducted a hearing test and determined that I had lost over 60% of my hearing in my right ear. *Man, what a really big sneeze.*

I asked what we could do for treatment, and the answer was time. Just wait for the eardrum to heal and see what hearing loss remained. Over time, I recovered a bit of my hearing, getting back to a little more than 50% normal hearing levels. At least now I had a legitimate reason to tell my wife I couldn't hear her. HA.

PERSONAL LEARNING POINT – Never block a sneeze. It's better to wake up everyone in the house (including the dog) than permanently damage your ear and lose your hearing. Trust me.

FILL THE GAP AND BE A PART OF THE SOLUTION

Back to business. As we started to turn the company's performance around and increase our development activity, including drilling more wells and building more platforms, we needed more staff. Until we were able to build in-country capability, in many cases, this meant more expatriate staff needed to be recruited. Historically, the company had an outstanding reputation for recruiting staff. While a bit remote from Europe and the Americas, the quality of life and amenities of the company camp were attractive to many potential staff who might move to Brunei.

After posting our first round of job openings, we were having a positive response from staff located in other areas around the world. Historically, when a new expat arrived in the country, they would spend a couple of weeks in a hotel until their "permanent" housing could be finalized. This short duration stay in temporary accommodation had never really been a problem before. However, as the number of new staff arriving each month increased, the short-duration stays started getting longer and longer. The bottleneck was the availability of move-in-ready houses. There were houses available, but they needed updates/repairs when the previous tenants moved out. The overall process was taking almost six months from departure to reoccupation for minor repairs (cleaning, painting, minor patching) to almost twelve months for major repairs (roof and/or floor replacement). The administrative parts of the process were taking almost three months of that time frame.

After six months of recruitment, we were approaching the vacancy limit in the local hotels. The non-working family members were getting frustrated as they drove through the camp and saw vacant houses while they were cramped in small hotel rooms with kids and having to continually dine out. The frustration was also seeping into the work production of the new staff as they spent time during the workday dealing with a disappointed spouse, which led to more time being spent with HR begging for a house. While the housing repair and allocation process did not fall to me, I was responsible for recruiting most of the new staff. A side effect of the housing delay was that our global reputation as a coveted posting was quickly eroding, and we were having difficulty recruiting top talent.

I had a choice. I could just sit back and accept the way things worked and try to lessen the frustration of the staff, or I could "help" find a solution. One week, after spending a good part of my time listening to the complaints from staff, I knew I had to act. I asked for a meeting with the Managing Director – MD (expat) and HR Director – HD (Bruneian). Rather than dump the problem on them, I outlined the issues, highlighted the growing costs to housing expenses (and company reputation), underlying causes, and recommended path forward. Not wanting to make this an expat-versus-national issue, I proposed that one of my Bruneian managers lead a process improvement design team.

This individual was not associated with any of the steps of the housing process, which made him impartial. At the same time, he was very inquisitive and was always seeking ways to improve work processes. He was a natural to lead the project. With the approval of the rest of the executive team, I served as the sponsor for the project. I met with the project lead to outline the issue and set the deliverables. The charge was to think of our housing stock and the turnover time between occupants like a landlord. The downtime when any house was vacant was really costing the company money. The goal was to complete minor repair turnarounds in less than a month and complete major repair turnarounds in less than three months. This would represent an 80% improvement from our most recent performance.

The leader was excited about the opportunity and commenced the evaluation of the existing process, identifying areas of delay and waste. With added construction crews and early design changes, in the first three months, we were able to start getting the families that had been stuck in temporary housing into their assigned homes. This outcome was a tremendous result. We had a lot of happy families and employees. By the end of six months, we had hit our targets. The minor repairs were finishing the turnaround in around three weeks, between one family exiting and another moving in. The major repairs were finishing the turnaround in a little over two months. Overall, it was a great success for the company, the expat families, and the project leader.

LEARNING POINT – When you see problems, you can either point them out and complain, or you can step up to help solve the problem. Be a part of the solution, not a part of the problem.

LIVING IN A FISHBOWL – EVERY ACTION MATTERS

As a member of the executive team at the largest commercial employer in the country, I was often surprised by comments from some employees in the organization. I mentioned previously that I had a company car and driver for trips around the country. However, on the weekends, I was on my own, but still in my company car. One weekend, I made a trip to run some errands in the capital, Bandar Seri Begawan, roughly 70 miles away at the other end of the country. I remembered my vehicle had a tracking device, so I made sure to follow the speed limit. After completing my errands, I made it back home by late afternoon in time for dinner at the employee club, sitting by the beach.

The following Monday, I was in a meeting with a group that reported to one of the other executive team members. After the meeting, one of the employees told me that they had seen me and my car in the parking area of one of the stores I had visited in the capital. I was very surprised as I didn't really interact with that employee that much, and they reported to another director. At that point, it really felt like I was living in a fishbowl. I realized that in my role, I was visible to others all the time. This was a little unsettling.

After some reflection, I also realized that it was a great responsibility. I needed to be on my best behavior, in both my actions and my words, wherever I went. It meant that in my actions at work and at play, I had to demonstrate the standard of performance for others. If I was curt or off-putting, then it meant others would think that they could do that as well. If I took shortcuts or didn't follow safety rules, then others would feel they could do the same. I learned that every one of my actions mattered. I had to live the life and follow the rules that I asked others to do. I couldn't rely on the old adage "Do as I say, not as I do." Instead, I had to live a life of "Follow my lead."

LEARNING POINT – As a senior leader, your words and actions matter. You set the standard for acceptable behavior. Set the standard high and live up to it.

BUILDING TALENT

After stabilizing the company's performance and addressing the housing shortage, we were successfully recruiting expat staff to fill vacancies and many critical leadership roles. The expat recruits were often top talent in the whole global organization. Many came from other expat postings, while some were in their first expat role. While the recruitment success was encouraging, in discussions with other executive team members, we agreed that expat recruitment was not sustainable as the long-term solution from both a cost standpoint and from a country staff development perspective, particularly for supervisor and leadership roles.

During a strategic direction exercise, each executive team member took an action to focus on developing future leaders from both the national staff and high-potential expats. As the Technical Director and with accountability for most of the technical staff in the company, I took this task to heart. In reviewing our leadership roster, we noticed that a majority of the technical leadership roles were held by expats. I challenged each of my leaders to identify their top talent. We developed career path models demonstrating steps on how an individual could build out their skill sets, broaden their perspective, and move into supervisor, management, and senior leadership roles. (Who knew that this was the start to my views of a Career Tree?)

While the career path models were a great starting point, they wouldn't mean much without further support. Once we had identified top talent, my leadership teams developed technical coaches and mentors for leadership skills. I also set an annual goal for each of my leaders (and their leaders) to serve as a mentor and coach to at least one emerging talent individual. We wanted to increase the number of national staff in supervisor and management roles in the technical and operations organization. We started moving staff (nationals and expats) into roles to stretch and strengthen their capabilities. Also, the progress on staff development became a part of our performance reviews for all leaders.

To jump-start the senior leadership focus, I asked each of my expat leaders who they could see in their organization doing their job in the future. Once the individuals were identified, we then started identifying gaps and actions that could be taken to close the gaps. Sometimes it meant moving a high-performing individual out of our organization to another group to accelerate their growth as a leader. The first couple of times this came up for discussion, there was some hesitation on the part of the "giving" leader. After discussions about the company's vision to develop national leaders capable of guiding it into the future, these moves became easier to facilitate. Alignment on the "greater good" became an enabler for commitment across the organization to leadership development.

For my own accountability, I wanted to start the development of specific national staff to take on my role on the executive team. The challenge was that we didn't have anyone immediately ready, as we had a limited number of national staff in senior manager roles in the technical and operational groups. This meant that getting someone to the Technical Director role would require a multi-step process that would take several years. Working with my fellow directors, we acknowledged the challenges and started taking the necessary steps. One of the first was to move some leaders around between leadership roles and even one of our most high-potential national staff out of the company (and country) to a role with a bigger scope.

While the conversation above suggests that staff and leadership development focused only on national staff, this was not the case. The process applied to expat staff who showed leadership potential. The challenge for the senior leadership and executive team was to strike the right balance. We made some progress during my time in Brunei, with both national and expat staff moving into new leadership roles.

In looking back now, I am extremely pleased and proud of how our efforts turned out. There were several expats who started their leadership journeys as an outgrowth of the development program. They went on to have outstanding careers. We had helped them **branch out** in the mid-career period and move toward **growing in stature** for bigger roles in their late-career period. And the national staff individual we moved out of the country? Yes, he became the first Bruneian to hold the Technical Director role on the executive team.

LEARNING POINT – Developing future leaders is a true sign of success for a senior executive. Usually, you lead an organization for only a few years. To position an organization for long-term success, you have to identify and develop the leaders who will follow after you. It is a daunting and challenging task, yet an awesome opportunity.

THE ROLE OF A LEADER (AND IT'S NOT WHAT YOU THINK)

As my time in the Technical Director role progressed, I became more comfortable with the duties of the role. I had seen some wins over the first few years:

- The new organization was in place to focus on the early development phases of oil and gas projects.
- The housing crisis for expat staff had been resolved, with incoming staff and their families spending minimal time in the local hotels before moving into their houses in the company camp.
- The company school had grown to accommodate the increased student count as the expat staff count grew. A new headmaster had been recruited, and new teachers were being brought on board as well. Parents were pleased with the quality of the education we were provided.
- The leaders on my team and in the technical ranks in the other parts of the company were growing their skills and becoming better leaders.
- Platforms were being built in the country to bring on new offshore fields.

Overall, the organization had changed the trajectory of its past performance and was well on the way to being globally recognized for delivering top performance in safety, production, costs, and technical quality.

In discussions with a couple of my key leaders, I came to a stark realization. On paper, the organization chart looked like a typical hierarchy pyramid, with me at the top and the 1200+ employees and contractors spread out across multiple levels below, but that wasn't the best way to think about the keys to success. While I could sit in my office issuing commands and demanding perfect execution, I most likely would not get the results (short and long term) that I wanted and expected. I had come to the realization that teams and the organization as a whole worked much better when I spent my time engaging with them. The time was spent sharing the *why* behind desired actions and goals, and asking about the pain points and bottlenecks they experienced in going about their day-to-day tasks.

In reality, the organization worked best when I "inverted" the work structure pyramid and realized that I really worked for 1200+ people. When the teams succeeded, I succeeded. I finally understood what being a servant leader meant. My time as a senior executive was better spent helping provide clarity and remove obstacles to success, rather than issuing commands from on high. While I had always been seen as a leader who engaged with his staff, my approach now had a whole new meaning.

LEARNING POINT – Your success as a senior executive isn't measured by how many commands you issue. A true measure of success is how effective you are at getting an organization aligned and at removing obstacles and barriers to let the organization work better. Start engaging with your staff. Ask for feedback. Become the servant leader.

STANDING TALL

The oil and gas industry was (and is) a primary driver of the national economy in Brunei and had been for decades. However, as one of the smallest countries in SE Asia, the available hydrocarbon resources for development and production were finite. Technology advances helped the company access some hard-to-reach resources, but more was needed to sustain performance for decades forward.

The executive team and key leaders from across the organization met in a series of visioning and strategy workshops, planning for the future of the company. We were looking beyond the standard 5-year planning window and testing all ideas on opportunities to add reserves to help sustain production performance for 10 to 20 years. We identified new areas for exploration and appraisal, along with areas where we could apply existing technologies used elsewhere in the industry that had not been put into practice in the company.

Each of the ideas had technical and economic challenges to immediately implement. The strategy group prioritized the ideas and then allocated the resources to mature the ideas through the development funnel. In reviewing the ideas, a few stood out for their sizeable potential for additional volumes. However, many of those also had higher technical and economic risks to project execution and profitability. These technical and economic risk areas become focus areas for the project teams to address. The global project maturation process included a series of reviews (tollgates) to assess the technical and commercial viability of development options. The overall timeline to move a project from the initial Identification phase through to Project Definition and then Final Investment

Decision ranged in time from 2 to 4+ years, depending on the complexities of each project. Given the company's corporate structure in Brunei, the decision to progress the projects through the tollgates resided with the Technical Director, namely me.

One of the largest opportunities was to install improved recovery methods, namely waterflooding, in some of the largest offshore producing fields in the country. While the potential upside was enticing, the technical challenges (both subsurface and field infrastructure) were complex. As a result, the early economic analysis indicated that the commercial viability of the project was weak. The asset team had been studying the possible development concept for a couple of years and was making slow but steady progress. At the start of the 4th year of my assignment, the global CEO visited Brunei. In discussions with the CEO and MD, I gave an overview of the funnel of projects under review for future development, including the large waterflood. I outlined the status of each along with the identified challenges. While noting the challenges, the waterflood project lead and I committed to progress through the first major tollgate by early Q2. This meant identifying at least one development scenario that could generate a small profit with reasonable recovery, cost, and pricing assumptions.

During Q2, we held the assurance review. Based on the feedback from the review team, I supported the project moving to the next phase of study. We had met our commitment to the senior leadership on project progress. The next tollgate was more demanding and required a specific design option that met defined minimum economic criteria, and could take over 24 months for a project this complex. We estimated that the teams could be ready for the next tollgate in 16 to 18 months, with additional staff. This would be a very tough timeline. The team needed to evaluate several diverse options to determine the most viable development scenario in a short period of time.

Around mid-year, the CEO visited again for some meetings with the government. During a review of the waterflood project, he requested that the project go through the next tollgate by year-end, significantly faster than similar projects around the world, and twice as fast as our accelerated plan. I outlined the challenges highlighted in the previous assurance review and actions underway to accelerate the next tollgate. With the additional staff, the team was making progress addressing the technical design challenges, and a preferred design option was emerging.

The CEO made a 3rd visit to the country in Q4. I was given a strong challenge to move the project through the next tollgate by year-end. I said that the team staff had been augmented and was making significant progress. I said it was likely that we would meet or even exceed our accelerated schedule, but we would not be able to pass the next tollgate as the project did not meet the globally defined criteria for moving forward. The CEO was not pleased, but I was not going to move forward with a project that wasn't yet technically or commercially viable.

After returning from our Christmas and New Year's holiday to Tasmania and then Sydney to see the New Year's Eve fireworks, I got the feeling that something had changed. It seemed like my engagements with the MD had taken a different tone. I just kept doing my job, focused on progressing the major projects, ensuring safe execution of our exploration, drilling, and construction projects, continuing to oversee the services (housing, schooling, transportation) for our expat staff and families, and coordinating the overall production and development plans for the year.

At the end of Q1, my daughter was excited because she had seen that a new American was coming to her school. When she told me the name, I knew that my replacement had been chosen without me being informed. The next day, I asked the MD if I was being replaced. He said nothing was formal. He indicated that I had completed four years in the role, which was longer than many previous Technical Directors. When I asked what was next for me, he said he didn't know. The global company was reorganizing, but no role had been designated for me. I left the meeting feeling dejected and a bit anxious. I told my wife what was happening. We spent many nights in the coming months walking along the beach of the South China Sea, discussing our options and praying for the path forward.

By May, I was informed that I was indeed being replaced, but that I needed to stay through the end of the summer until the new leader was able to move in country. It broke my heart to have to tell my kids that we were being transferred back to Houston. My daughter was devastated because she would be returning home for her senior year of high school and would miss her final year in Brunei, particularly the planned Duke of Edinburgh Gold Award activities with her friends from the past four years. My wife and I cancelled our planned 25th anniversary trip to a Malaysian tea plantation. Instead, we flew to Houston to find a house. It's amazing how you can find a house, get inspections, and sign a final contract in five days. We were also the first people with our title company to do a house closing from 12,000 miles away. It might be common now but was truly unique in 2009.

As the school year finished, my daughter went back to the US in June to spend time with her grandparents and get her driver's license. My wife and son left in early July to start getting the house ready to move in. I was trying to be strong, even as I had concerns about my career future. I did not have a specified role awaiting me. I had been unsuccessful in securing a position in the global reorganization. It seemed odd given the feedback and high individual performance numbers I had received in each of the years I had been in the TD role, including the year I departed. I left Brunei in late August 2009 to spend four weeks of accumulated PTO. I had instructions to report to the Houston office at the end of September, but there was still no defined role. My anxiety meter was continuing to climb. I was still 20 months away from early retirement.

LEARNING POINT – When your integrity is challenged, you can cave or you can stand tall, even if there are personal impacts.

BACK TO THE US, BUT WHAT NEXT?

In late September, I reported to the Houston Exploration and Production office. After meeting with several members of the Regional Executive Leadership Team (RELT), I was given an assignment supporting the RELT members on any special projects they may have. It felt like a "filler" job, but I promised myself and the RELT that I would do my best, and they would not be disappointed.

Over the next several months, I worked on projects helping create programs for Asset Integrity on the FPSO (Floating Production Storage and Offloading) vessels in Brazil and Health, Safety, and Environment (HSE) management systems for the Region. The GMs and executive team members were very excited about the work products. Imagine my surprise when my assigned RELT "supervisor" told me that my year-end performance rating was "Failing to meet expectations" after having left Brunei with an "Exceeds Expectations" rating.

I was now on the potential discharge list, and with no permanent role, I wasn't sure how much longer I would be employed. I could have checked out and coasted, but I had made a commitment to the RELT to support them. I wasn't one to go back on my commitments. The Regional President thanked me for my work so far and indicated that there were further projects that could use my expertise while he looked for a more permanent role for me. I thanked him for his confidence and jumped into the next special project. I continued to work the Asset Integrity and HSE programs. My biggest project was serving as the technical advisor for a field sale package in the Gulf of Mexico, primarily of deepwater fields. This was a fun activity, similar to the work I had done back in 2003 during my last assignment in New Orleans. Helping the teams highlight the opportunities with each of the potential bidding companies was positioning the package for a top bid.

After much prayer and consideration, given the uncertainty of any future permanent role and each month bringing me closer to my early retirement date, I started considering working for other companies. I felt that moving to a mid-sized independent oil and gas company would be the best fit for my experience and expertise. After reviewing the industry, I selected five companies I would consider for my next career move. In Q2 2010, I had an interview with my preferred choice. The proposed role was a step up from my Technical Director role in Brunei. It was a slight stretch, but I felt I could do it. After a couple of face-to-face interviews with members of the executive leadership team, I was informed that I was unsuccessful. The feedback was that there was another individual more qualified. They also said that they were impressed with my background and would keep me in mind for future roles that might open up. I thanked them and went back to supporting the field sales team. Over the next few months, the sales package was presented to prospective buyers with some solid interest.

On the home front, our daughter graduated from high school and was preparing to head off to university to study environmental engineering. It was a great celebration with both sets of grandparents coming to see her graduate. A couple of weeks later, I was sitting at work reviewing some papers and got a call from my middle sister. She said that our dad had taken himself to the hospital with a case of pneumonia. I was concerned but not overly anxious. The next morning, she called back and said he had taken a turn for the worse, and I should come back to Mississippi to see him. I told my boss, went home to pack some clothes, and started the 8-hour drive to Meridian, Mississippi. That was the longest drive of my life, at least emotionally. I prayed for Dad's healing all the way home. And I feared the worst with the possibility of losing a guide/mentor/life coach looming over my thoughts.

Dad continued to decline over the next two days. There wasn't anything we could do. His body couldn't fight the pneumonia. Our focus was also on Mom, as she was not in the best of health and was about to lose her partner of 55 years. That weekend, on Father's Day, we all gathered around him and prayed as he passed away. That day will continue to hold a special memory for me as my earthly father went to be with his Heavenly Father.

REPEAT LEARNING POINT – Life can change suddenly. Pursue the things you love, both in your work and your life.

I had lost my role model, first mentor, and personal advisor. While he had never attended college, he was one of the smartest men I knew, and he lived his life to serve others. He passed along the traits of "do your best" and "put others first." While I had forgotten the latter part in my early career, as I was contemplating my future professional career, his advice came back full force. Six weeks later, the independent oil and gas company called back and said they had a role for me if I wanted it. I went in to learn more about the role and have a set of cursory interviews to confirm that the company and I were a match for each other. I was excited for the opportunity and started planning my departure from the company where I had worked for the past 28 years.

Shortly after Labor Day, I made a trip to New Orleans to celebrate a successful field sale with the team. We had received a purchase price above our minimum bid. Everyone was elated. After the celebration, while talking to the project lead, I got a call from the Regional President. He said that he had been successful in getting me "cleared" to take a permanent executive role. It would be a step down to start but would put me back in play for future bigger roles. I expressed my deep appreciation for all that he had done for me. I also told him that I had been offered and accepted a role with an independent oil and gas company. I told him that I had planned to stop by the next day when I was back in Houston to give him my notice and close out my existing projects. When I stopped by the next morning, I got his support for my planned departure and his best wishes for my new position. At my departure two weeks later, I was informed that I had once again "Exceeded Expectations" with my support of the RELT the past year and would be rewarded accordingly. I was very happy to be departing on good terms with my colleagues.

My career with Shell was coming to a close after 28 years, with my early retirement. I had given Shell my best, achieved some outstanding results, and helped develop and grow many future technical advisors and organization leaders. I was ready to move to the next chapter and make my mark at a new company.

LEARNING POINT – Life and work both come with ups and downs. To position yourself for success throughout the hills and valleys, do your best, keep your word, and serve others.

LOOKING BACK WITH SOME VINDICATION

Fast forward to 2019, 10 years after I left Brunei in 2009. I had recently retired for the second time, and we were planning our move back to New Orleans, where my professional career started. One day, I got a LinkedIn message. The individual was leading an independent Post Investment Review (PIR) of the mega waterflood development project in Brunei. He requested an interview with me as a part of the review since I had been the executive overseeing the project during one of the early planning/tollgate phases. During the discussion of the results of the project, he shared that the review had been initiated as the project had not met expectations for volumes and profitability that had been set at the time of board approval. He said that the project had not fully delivered the predicted oil volumes, that costs had been higher than forecast, and that project milestones/timelines had been missed. Overall, the project had not returned the level of profitability presented to the board and government at project sanction.

As I had not been at the company for most of that time, I did not know how the project had performed after my departure. I shared with the interviewer that these were many of the same issues that were being studied at the time of my departure and the primary reasons why I had not rushed the project forward to the final two tollgates. He appreciated the background of the early phases of the project and incorporated my feedback into the company report. For myself, I felt some vindication for the decisions and actions I had taken, even if they had led to my departure from Brunei and from Shell.

+++++++++++++++++++++

This chapter has focused on my transition to a senior executive role and taking an international assignment. I have shared learnings on understanding different cultures and on how your personal style can impact your effectiveness in them. I also shared about spending time developing others, how to respond to adversity, and maybe most importantly, NEVER BLOCK A SNEEZE.

160

For those who may find themselves starting a senior executive role, you should consider:

- Understanding your personal behavior style and the culture of the organization and country where you work.
- Focusing the organization to both deliver current performance while mapping the vision for the future.
- Realizing that your minimal performance is the best you can expect from others. You set the standard for acceptable performance.
- Understanding your personal values
- Building personal resilience to overcome career and life setbacks

REFLECTION QUESTIONS:

- Is my personal style effective in the new organization? If not, does the organization change, or do I need to?
- What standard of performance have I set for myself, and thus the organization, in terms of focus, delivery, safety, commitment to others, and work-life balance?
- How do my actions and interactions demonstrate the values I hold?
- What am I doing to define the organization's future vision, including developing the leaders of tomorrow?
- How will I respond to setbacks? Do I fold and give up? Or do I stand tall on my values and principles and prepare for a better tomorrow?

SUMMARY OF LEARNING POINTS – GOING GLOBAL

- If you find yourself in an area (or country) with different customs, don't just "trust your instincts." Be willing to take guidance from those more knowledgeable.

- Being a senior leader doesn't mean you have to isolate yourself. At the same time, it doesn't mean that you are best friends with all your staff. Finding the balance between leader and friend can be challenging. Learning to segregate the two aspects of your life, and being humble in both, makes each role easier.

- As you take on more senior executive roles, you will find yourself accountable for areas of the business where you don't have expertise. It is critical to leverage the experience and expertise of other leaders on your team. Your job is to put in place the policies, practices, and support systems to help your team succeed.

- A lack of knowledge of national culture can lead to missteps. Be aware and be knowledgeable about cultural norms. You may very well avoid embarrassment from putting your foot in your mouth.

- National culture trumps personal style. Be prepared to change your approach or accept frustration and delays. You may find that the change in approach alters your leadership style for years to come. Your adaptability will also be a role model for other leaders in your organization, helping them navigate their own development.

- REPEAT – Life can change suddenly. Pursue the things you love, both in your work and your life.

- When faced with a new and unfamiliar environment, you can retreat into your shell and close off others, or you can take the (tough) step to put yourself out there, engaging with others, and build new relationships (and even friendships).

- PERSONAL – Never block a sneeze. It's better to wake up everyone in the house (including the dog) than permanently damage your ear and lose your hearing. Trust me.

- When you see problems, you can either point them out and complain, or you can step up to help solve the problem. Be a part of the solution, not a part of the problem.

- As a senior leader, your words and actions matter. You set the standard for acceptable behavior. Set the standard high and live up to it.

- Developing future leaders is a true sign of success for a senior executive. Usually, you lead an organization for only a few years. To position an organization for long-term success, you have to identify and develop the leaders who will follow after you. It is a daunting and challenging task, yet an awesome opportunity.

- Your success as a senior executive isn't measured by how many commands you issue. A true measure of success is how effective you are at getting an organization aligned and at removing obstacles and barriers to let the organization work better. Start engaging with your staff. Ask for feedback. Become the servant leader.

- When your integrity is challenged, you can cave or you can stand tall, even if there are personal impacts.

- REPEAT – Life can change suddenly. Pursue the things you love, both in your work and your life.

- Life and work both come with ups and downs. To position yourself for success throughout the hills and valleys, do your best, keep your word, and serve others.

Chapter 9

Changing Companies – Starting Over and Proving Myself Again

After having planted my career seed, growing a strong functional trunk, and climbing my Career Tree for over 28 years at Shell, it was time to move to another company. While I had extensive experience and expertise, in some ways, it felt like starting over and having to prove myself again to new peers, staff, and leaders. Changing companies can be daunting. It felt like I had done some pruning of my Career Tree to position myself to grow again.

This chapter will explore the challenges and opportunities that come with changing companies, with emphasis on leveraging past skills to position yourself for success, being true to your personal values, committing to help others grow even as you grow yourself, continuing your learning journey, and preparing the way for future success.

STARTING OVER

After 28 years at one company, starting at a new company felt, in some ways, like I had just graduated from university and was starting my professional career over again. While I had held many roles in different cities and countries with Shell, they were all with the same company. This was truly starting over.

I took a couple of weeks off between jobs. I jokingly say that I went to work for my wife, and she was the toughest boss I ever had. She had a close friend from our time in Brunei who was coming over to visit for a few weeks, and they were going to stay at our cabin in the Texas hill country, sewing and visiting. My job was to make sure everything was in working order. I was sent to spruce things up and make sure it was spic and span. After completing everything on the list in a couple of days, I was feeling good and felt I could relax a little. That's when my wife told me the rest of the list that needed to be done. I think she was worried that if she gave me the full list at one time, I might balk. When I got back home after finishing everything on the list, I told her that I needed to find a real job, since her definition of work was physical labor, and my definition was not. Luckily, that real job was starting in a week. I was exhausted and excited.

A WORLDWIDE TEAM

My new job was as a senior subsurface manager at the petroleum organization for BHP Billiton. While BHP Billiton was more readily known as one of the largest mining companies in the world, the Petroleum division would have been one of the larger independent oil and gas companies if it had been a standalone company. An interesting difference for the Petroleum division was that the leaders had come from many of the majors in the industry. As such, the company culture was a blend of many of the aspects of other companies. The expectation was that leaders brought the best of their companies to BHP Billiton while leaving the baggage behind.

Another difference was that the leadership structure and team makeup were fairly lean compared to those of larger companies. As such, the expectation was for individuals to carry a heavy load.

The job was a newly created role consolidating the subsurface teams supporting the oil and gas activities and operations in Pakistan, UK – Liverpool Bay, Trinidad and Tobago, and overseeing the non-operated fields in Algeria. I had team members in the US, UK, Pakistan, and Trinidad. I was excited to be supporting international operations again. The team had a wide range of specialties, including geologists, geophysicists, reservoir engineers, and production engineers. While I had senior staff in each location, it was a large team, all reporting to me. A big job, but I was super excited.

When I was recruited for the role, the executive team highlighted the challenges of the new position. The fields had not received strong technical support in recent years and needed technical focus to improve performance understanding and enhance future production. I would also need to combine teams from around the world, support three General Managers, while only reporting to one. The President of Production also indicated that, while the role was not at the Senior Executive level, it required someone with that level of experience. I knew the role was a little smaller than my previous technical director role, but the future growth opportunities and the culture of the new company were what convinced me to take it. I was ready to get started.

LEARNING POINT – Sometimes you have to take a step back to position yourself for future growth. Also, in looking at new opportunities and companies, remember that company culture is a key value for determining your fit in an organization. In some cases, it even trumps compensation.

GETTING STARTED AND BUILDING CONNECTIONS

I arrived at the new office, eager to get started. I met with the team members based in Houston and started learning about their roles and the fields they supported. During my first few weeks, we also arranged video meetings with the staff based in Islamabad, Pakistan; Conwy, Wales; and Port of Spain, Trinidad. Introductions over a computer screen are difficult, but I focused on learning a bit about each individual, hearing about the work they were doing, and the challenges they were facing. I shared a bit of my background and my ways of working. My primary objective was not to shake things up but instead to make a connection before having a chance to meet in person.

I scheduled similar sessions with my three "bosses," the General Managers/country leads for Pakistan, the UK, and Trinidad. As mentioned previously, this was a bit tricky as I reported to the UK leader but was expected to effectively support all three. The focus on these leader sessions was sharing and learning about each other, and just as important, learning the pain points of what had not worked in the prior organization model, areas where they needed support, and what success of the new organization meant to them. While I would have preferred to visit with each leader and team member in person, making the early connections helped build effective long-term working relationships.

168

LEARNING POINT – When stepping into a leadership role, a key to early success is building connections with your staff, your direct leader, and the other leaders in the organization you will be interfacing with. These connections are the foundation of effective engagement and support.

LIFE HAPPENS, AND CULTURE MATTERS

I had spent my first month connecting with my staff and the three country leaders. As we entered the month of November, I was preparing to make my first round of trips to visit each location. I was sitting in a leadership team meeting reviewing recent performance across the company when I got a call from my oldest sister. She said that our mom wasn't doing well, and I need to travel to Florida as soon as possible to see her. After my dad's death in June, since none of the kids lived close enough to take care of her each day, Mom had moved to an assisted living facility in Florida, where my sister worked as one of the senior nursing staff. This allowed my sister to check in with Mom each day and monitor the care she was receiving. Even so, she had been declining ever since Dad's passing.

When I got off the call, I asked the President of the Production organization if I could speak to him for a moment. He paused the field performance review meeting and came over to talk. I explained the situation with my mom and that I needed to travel to Florida to see her. I said that I would have to postpone my trips to the fields, and I might be out for a couple of weeks, depending on her outcome. Since I had only been at the company for a month or so, I was a little nervous. I had not built up a bank of PTO. He was immediately supportive and said to take all the time I needed. He said that he would communicate with the country leads and explain why my travel was being postponed. I was so relieved. I was also pleased as his support reaffirmed my choice of company to work for.

I booked my flight to Florida and arrived the next day. I got to see Mom for a couple of days before she passed away. I called my wife and kids and let them know. I also called the office and gave them the update on Mom's passing. Again, everyone was extremely supportive, from my team to the country leads to the executive team. They reaffirmed the guidance to stay as long as I needed to help my sister settle my mom's affairs and for the funeral that would take place back in Mississippi. The company's support was reaffirmed just two months later when my father-in-law passed away unexpectedly. The prayers, support, and encouragement from my team and the company leadership were uplifting. I knew I was in the right place.

REPEAT LEARNING POINT – Life can change suddenly. Pursue the things you love, both in your work and your life.

LEARNING POINT – As both an employee and a leader, company culture matters. Building relationships with each other and supporting each other in your time of need speaks volumes. When you feel supported, your commitment and effort are strengthened.

DIVERSE TEAMS – ALL AROUND THE WORLD

After the deaths of three parents/grandparents in a little over six months, our family was a bit shaken. We each returned to our individual activities to regain a sense of normalcy, be it school, volunteering, or work. For me, it was restarting my connections with my dispersed team and the three country leaders. I started making my trips to the various countries to meet the teams face-to-face.

Through these interactions, I came to appreciate my international assignment with Shell even more. My experience working with individuals from a variety of countries was paying off as I began engaging with staff, leaders, and partners for operations in Pakistan, the UK, and Trinidad and Tobago. After the first round of visits, I noticed different styles for the team members in each country. This included the country leaders. For instance, the UK team was more open and direct, while the Pakistan team was more reserved and deferential.

Each of the countries my team supported had upcoming development projects and/or key decisions that needed approval and financial backing from the partners. The partners in each country came from around the world and often had differing priorities and objectives for the fields. My job was to gain alignment across the partners, including governmental agencies, and manage each project forward to its respective investment decision. From my global experience, I knew that each of these countries went about the decision-making process differently, often reflecting the cultural norms of their nation.

A great example was in Pakistan. On one of my first visits to the country, we had a partnership meeting to review current performance and discuss the possibility of further development of the field with additional wells to be drilled. The meeting was scheduled to last 4 hours. The local team leader had told me that past partner meetings were often very lengthy and difficult, with few decisions being made. He warned me that many of the representatives from the partners liked to express their opinions and often felt they had to get in the last word. At the start of the meeting, I gave a short overview of my bio and work history, emphasizing my technical background and leadership roles. After reviewing the current performance, I asked if there were any questions. Immediately, various attendees started speaking. I had to actively manage the room to ensure only one person spoke at a time. I now understood what the local leader meant about difficult meetings in the past.

The next (and primary) topic on the agenda was the upcoming development program to drill additional wells. This was more contentious as early indications were that not all the partners were aligned on the need for more wells. I had my work cut out for me in facilitating the session. After reviewing the technical basis for the recommended path forward of two additional wells, I reopened the meeting to questions and comments. Only this time, I was prepared. I went around the room asking a representative of each partner to express their views and any concerns. After each group spoke, I summarized their comments and captured key points, then asked them to confirm that I had accurately captured their position. I repeated this process for each partner group. At the end, I reviewed all comments and concerns, outlined the steps the technical team would take to address them, and provided a timeline for responding to the group. As we wrapped up the meeting, the local team leader said he had never seen the partners as aligned on the path forward. And, we didn't have to schedule another partner meeting in the next few months as had been the past experience. Yay, success!

We had similar results in the meetings with partners in the other countries. The teams were learning to be receptive to input from the partners and build relationships with the staff in those companies.

LEARNING POINT – When dealing with multiple partners/team members, it is critical to make sure everyone feels that their input was heard and considered. Your job as a leader is to create the environment to allow full input and to facilitate the group to reach consensus on the path forward.

WORLD EVENTS AND DIFFERENT PERSPECTIVES

A couple of months after the partner meeting in Pakistan, I made a trip back to meet with members of my team. I was traveling with the President of Production, the VP of Engineering, and another of our senior managers. When the trip was scheduled, I wondered why the senior executives were joining me. As we started, the President told me that during the trip, we were going to announce the promotion of the operations manager to the country lead. He would be the first Pakistani to hold the position in the country. The other senior manager in our traveling group was going to be the new operations manager.

After arriving in Pakistan, we had a big celebration for the new country lead with all the staff in the office. The leaders then spent time in handover sessions while I met with my Pakistan team members to discuss their work in support of the proposed additional wells.

Before we departed the following afternoon, we spent some time walking through portions of the Shakaparian National Park. It was interesting to see the beauty of the park and its national monuments through the eyes of the local leaders. It was also interesting to see the reactions of the other park visitors when they saw a group of four Caucasian men walking through the park. We had to cut our tour short to catch our charter flight early due to a forecast of fog that evening. After landing in Dubai, I caught my flight back to Houston. I was exhausted after spending more time flying back and forth than I had spent in Pakistan. I arrived back home just in time to celebrate my wife's birthday, so I did get some points in the "home office."

The following evening, my son came running in and said to check the news. There was a breaking story that the US had located and killed Osama bin Laden. Imagine my surprise that he had been found in Pakistan and just 20 miles from where we had been staying. I was also surprised to learn that the mission had been delayed by a day due to "weather" in the area. This was the same "weather" that caused us to depart early. On Monday morning, we had our global call-in for operations, with country leads from around the world discussing various aspects of their businesses. The President asked the new Pakistan country lead how the mood was in the country after the events of the weekend. He said that "after the assassination of bin Laden," the mood was tense but not violent. The words shocked me as the perspective of the Western world was that the events of the past weekend were a positive result. The words also highlighted how perspective impacts our view of the world.

LEARNING POINT – As a leader, you will often interact with others with different backgrounds and/or from different regions of the world. To enhance your leadership capability, you have to have an awareness and consideration of their viewpoints, even if they are different from yours. Considering multiple viewpoints is a strength to be developed.

KNOWING WHEN TO CUT YOUR LOSSES

The teams were evaluating plans for additional wells in each of the countries we supported. The Pakistan project was moving through partner discussions as mentioned previously. In Trinidad, we had gained support from the partners and were in the final stages of reaching internal approval for the program. The program included a couple of high-quality infill wells with no major risks. After a detailed review with the country lead and the VP of Engineering, we received support for an additional outstep well. The subsurface team had confidence in the analysis and felt that even though there was some geological and reservoir risk of failure, a successful outcome could open up potential new areas for production. We outlined the risks in the approval process while expressing confidence in the expected outcome.

The outstep well started drilling in December. We were reaching the target zones as the holiday approached. Not the best timing if we got unexpected results. While away on vacation, I got a call from the geologist saying we had reached the target zone with mixed results. The indicators said we should drill further. I alerted the senior leaders and gave the approval to drill ahead. As the drilling progressed, I got updates on the results every couple of hours. It made for a couple of long days and nights. Ultimately, after drilling for a few more days, the geologist reached the point where he could no longer support his original interpretation and said the target sands were not present, and the well was a failure. I relayed the outcome to the senior leaders, and we terminated and abandoned the well. I was disappointed in the outcome as I/we had sold it as having a fairly high chance of success. After reviewing the results, I had to ask the team and myself if we had been biased towards a successful outcome in our original analysis. I also told the country lead and VP of Engineering that I should have made the call to stop the drilling earlier. I didn't like being wrong or spending the capital funds that could have been used for other projects. Luckily, that well was the single disappointment for the drilling program.

LEARNING POINT – As a leader of an organization, when evaluating a proposal or investment, don't let your bias/hope for a successful outcome cloud your judgment of the value of the project. And don't chase the hope for a positive outcome for too long. Sometimes, it takes a failure to teach you how to better evaluate opportunities and prepare for future projects.

EXPERIENCE COUNTS

I really enjoyed my time working with team members and leaders around the world, helping improve our performance in each country. During my tenure in the role, I also picked up additional responsibilities (and staff) to cover the non-operated assets in the US Gulf and in offshore Australia. For me, this was exciting as I got to interact with more staff and expand my knowledge of the global portfolio. After a couple of years in the role, I was talking to one of the senior executives about future roles. He had not been involved in my initial interviews. Given my current role, he thought my background was predominantly in subsurface engineering. I gave a brief overview of the different roles I had held at Shell. He asked to see my resume. When we met again a couple of months later, we discussed the roles where I had operations and senior leadership responsibilities, particularly in West Texas, Michigan, the US Gulf, and overseas. I left thinking that at least another senior leader knew a bit more about my broad background.

LEARNING POINT – Building and broadening your skill set and experience can and will position you for future opportunities. Making sure others in leadership positions know your capabilities is also important. Don't sell yourself short, but at the same time, don't oversell your background. In the end, let your work speak for itself.

RETURNING TO MY ROOTS (AND GETTING WET)

I was pleasantly surprised when I was promoted to be the General Manager for the Gulf of Mexico a couple of months later. After two and a half years as the senior subsurface manager, I was eager to step back into a role leading a broad organization as the executive with accountability for technical, operational, safety, and financial performance.

In my normal method, I started my rounds of interacting with the various team members and leaders, learning about each individual and any pains or bottlenecks I could help with (see the upside-down organization pyramid discussion and servant leader Learning Point in Chapter 8). When talking to my operations manager, I realized that I needed to go visit the teams offshore as well.

But there was one problem. My HUET (Helicopter Underwater Evacuation Training) certificate had expired. In simple terms, the HUET training was focused on teaching you the skills to survive a helicopter ditching in open waters. Critically important if you were on hour-long trips 100+ miles offshore. We also liked to joke that going to HUET was being paid for a day spent half-drowned.

REPEAT LEARNING POINT – As a senior leader, your words and actions matter. You set the standard for acceptable behavior. Set the standard high and live up to it.

Let's just say the training day was long and wet. After a couple of hours in the morning on safety procedures and CPR training, we moved to the pool for the afternoon. The training takes place in an open cylinder capsule set up as a mock helicopter with a real seat and window configuration. With safety as a top priority, the exercises had two lifeguards in the capsule and divers in the water on either side. Six students went through each exercise together. Even though I had completed the training twice before (once as GM for the Gulf of Mexico and again as the Technical Director in Brunei), I was still a bit anxious. I can swim but have had a lifelong fear of drowning.

We would do five exercises to complete the training and get our certificate, which would be valid for four years. Two exercises would be straight dunkings, one with the windows out (easiest) and one with the windows in place. With the windows in place, you first had to bump the window out and then extract yourself from the capsule. The next two exercises would be upside down, one with the windows out and then with the windows in place (hardest). The final exercise was equally challenging. In this one, only four students were in the capsule at a time, as each student had to exit a window on the opposite side from where they were sitting while being dunked. Luckily, this last exercise was done while sitting upright and not upside down.

I was in the third group for each exercise. Some of the students did not know how to swim. In my view, they were very brave to do the training. While the first group was completing the exercise, I could feel my anxiety rising. When the second group was getting settled, I was talking to myself and trying to calm down. I tested myself and held my breath when they went under. When everyone was clear and back on the side, I was still holding my breath. I looked down and saw that it had taken less than 20 seconds.

OK, I can do this. I got myself into the capsule and found my seat. We got the final instructions from the lifeguard trainer, and we started to go under the water. As the water reached my chest, I took a deep breath, closed my eyes, and got ready to put my training into action. I counted to three like we had been told, to wait for the bubbles to clear, then unbuckled and moved towards the window. Halfway out the window, I was stuck. I couldn't go any further. WHAT WAS GOING ON? I AM GOING TO DROWN!!!! Fighting off the panic, with my eyes still closed, I felt down to my waist and found that the seatbelt had become wrapped around my life vest. I pulled the seat belt free, pushed through the window, and swam to the surface. The scuba diver came over to make sure I was fine. Once I was out of the pool, the trainer stopped by and said, "Good work." He told me he had seen the seatbelt get stuck and was about to come to my aid when I freed myself. With those words from the trainer and my own actions, I had a new confidence that I could complete the series of exercises. I was proud that I had not panicked. And with my certificate in hand, I was able to continue my engagement meetings and spent several days offshore over the next few weeks.

LEARNING POINT – Training isn't always easy or fun. But it is important. Never skip your training. You never know when the skills you learn may be called into action. And they may even help save your life.

KNOW YOUR STYLE & BE TRUE TO YOURSELF

During one of our annual strategy and planning exercises, the HR team led an effort to enhance the leadership capabilities of our entire organization. As a part of the process, they asked 24 of the top leaders in Petroleum (GMs, VPs, Chief Engineers/Geoscientists) to complete a Merrill and Reid Social Styles assessment. The intent was for us to better understand our own style of engagement, recognize the styles of others, and learn how to improve communication and collaboration between styles.

The four Social Styles were given labels (and colors):

- Driver (Red) – Action-oriented
- Analytical (Blue) – Process-oriented
- Expressive (Yellow) – Idea-oriented
- Amiable (Green) – People-oriented

Once completed, they brought us together to review the results. We had each received our individual results but did not know the outcome of the other leaders. After giving an overview

180

of the assessments and the characteristics of each style, the facilitator asked us to grab a corner based on our primary Social Style. Of the 24 leaders present, there were 12 Drivers (reasonable outcome given we were the top leaders in the organization), 10 Analytical (again, reasonable as most of the leaders came from a technical background), 1 Expressive (you probably guessed it – HR), and 1 Amiable (me). As we looked around the room, one of my colleagues who was in the Analytical corner pointed at me and said, "How the *hell* did you get in here?" He wasn't wrong. I was the outlier of the group. As we sat down, another colleague who had been in the Driver group leaned over and whispered, "I bet you are really a closet Driver." He was closer to the truth. The Driver style was tied for my second-highest score with the Analytical style. If you remember from Chapter 8, I had been a Driver style with an Analytical background prior to my international posting in Brunei but had modified my style when that approach had been ineffective in achieving results. It looked like 4+ years of modifying my style had stuck. You know what, I was glad. I liked the approach of engaging others, gaining alignment, and working to collectively deliver results. And over time, my colleagues came to appreciate the difference as well.

LEARNING POINT – As a senior leader, there is tremendous value in understanding your personality/behavior style, learning how to recognize other styles, and knowing how best to interact with other styles. Take time to do an assessment. A couple of my favorites are Merrill and Reid Social Styles and TTI Disc and Driving Forces.

EMERGING TALENT (AT MULTIPLE LEVELS)

When I took over the GM role, the various manager roles were already filled, along with my Asset Planner role. In a sense, I had inherited my leadership team. The question was: do I keep them in their roles or change the leaders out? Having been in the situation of being the established manager when a new GM comes onboard, I knew the concern each of them felt. I knew they wanted me to give them a chance. I met with each one of them to let them know they would be staying in their position.

I also outlined my ways of working, which included meeting with them early in their assignment to set and align on the expectations of the role and their personal goals. At that point, I would step back to let them lead their teams. I would always be available to give guidance and address any issues they thought were beyond the scope of their role. I would not be checking in each and every day, nor asking to be involved in every decision they made. I also told them they would know when they were not meeting my expectations, as I would default to giving them specific tasks to deliver. This would be an obvious change from my style of letting them set the actions and pace of work for their teams. It would also be a point where I expected them to come to me to discuss where they were missing the mark. Each person was eager to give it a go.

Over the next several months, I did make a change or two to the makeup of my leadership team as a couple of individuals did not perform well when given the broader latitude (and expectation) of setting work scope, deliverables, and pace for their team, even with additional coaching from me. On the flip side, I was pleased to see several leaders take the opportunity to grow their own skills and position themselves to climb further in their Career Tree. Following my commitment to being a servant leader, I really invested in my direct reports and their teams. In particular, I sought the input of my leaders on key decisions, particularly on forecast performance from the existing fields, capital programs for new wells, and key technical studies. While final decisions on targets (capital and operating budgets and production volumes) were mine alone, I wanted the team to have input and then to understand the rationale behind the final numbers. In the end, with their input, I made informed decisions regarding key metrics for our asset.

I was also very encouraged to see the managers and my Asset Planner start to do the same with their teams. They started coming to budget and planning sessions with a broader perspective. As we continued to meet, they began to anticipate my questions and even started challenging themselves to consider all options. For me, this was exhilarating. I was seeing future talent emerge from across the organization. Several individuals were building the skills and broadening their perspectives to become future leaders.

Over the following years, I was very proud to see some of the managers successfully move to Executive roles and some of the junior staff move to management roles. They continue to climb their own Career Trees and work on mentoring and developing the staff and leaders on their own teams and their own companies.

LEARNING POINT – As a leader, take time to invest in your people. Their personal and professional growth is one measure of your own effectiveness as a leader. It can also be personally fulfilling to see their continued success.

THE VALUE OF ALIGNED OBJECTIVES

For our largest offshore field in the Gulf of Mexico, Shenzi, the company was using waterflooding of key reservoirs to improve the oil recovery. From a technical perspective, this meant injecting treated seawater deep underground to help sweep oil to the producers. This recovery approach was a proven method across the Gulf but was not without risk, both from subsurface uncertainty and the very high cost of the injection wells.

Prior to my appointment as the GM, the Asset team had drilled a couple of new injection wells. However, when the injection started, the rates for the wells were a fraction of the modeled rates. Technical reviews indicated damage around the injection point. Further analysis showed that the drilling and completion (D&C) activities and fluids could have been better controlled, particularly over the injection zone. During discussions among the teams, we identified misalignment on key goals. The D&C teams were primarily focused on safely executing the wells as quickly and cost-effectively as possible. This wasn't hard to understand and appreciate when the drilling rig costs often exceeded $1 million per day, and wells could take 2 or 3 months to drill and complete. The subsurface teams were focused on maximizing injection rates, as this would increase oil recovery. However, the joint reviews indicated that the fast D&C activities were severely limiting injection rates.

The subsurface teams identified that more injection wells were needed, given additional recovery opportunities and the poor performance of the recent injection wells. But just replicating the past results would not be acceptable or profitable. **So, what next?** At the encouragement of myself and the VP of Drilling, the two teams worked together to redesign the D&C activities across the injection zones. They agreed on steps to control the drilling rate and fluid quality during the final stages of the well. The changes would result in a longer time to finish the well, and thus a higher capital cost, but the improved oil production would be worth the additional investment. With the two teams' aligned objectives, a joint recommendation was made to senior leaders and partners to drill another injection well. It was a tough sell but was ultimately approved. We put the well on the drill schedule. As the rig activity started, everyone on the Asset and D&C teams carefully watched the execution of the well. The D&C met their commitments on the well and delivered within the revised time and budget numbers. The field team connected the flowlines and made the well ready for injection.

Now came the real test. Could we do better than the previous wells and ultimately achieve the desired injection rates? After a couple of days, we did get higher rates than the early injectors. The first test was successfully passed. Over the next few weeks, the field team continued to ramp up injection rate. At the end, collectively, we exceeded the designed target injection rate. YAY. The second test was successfully passed. Now, could we sustain injection? Over the next several months, the injection rate stayed steady. We also started to see signs that the oil production was stabilizing. The redesign of the injection wells had reopened opportunities for further wells and additional recovery. The teams had gone from failure to success by working together. A big win for the teams and the company.

LEARNING POINT – Misaligned objectives often result in subpar results. As a senior leader, your charge is to encourage teams to work together to reach an agreement on aligned objectives. This alignment is critical to position the organization for success. Get the teams working together, then step back and watch them exceed your expectations.

The Asset teams were working together to improve the performance of the fields and deliver value to the company. We were gaining a growing reputation in the deepwater sector of the Gulf of Mexico, one of the few independent oil and gas companies that were positioned to compete with the majors.

I was excited about the work the teams were doing and where we could go. In one of my monthly reviews with the VP for Conventional Production, we were reviewing the performance of the Asset and plans for the future. As I brought up the future plans, the VP stopped me and said, "Let's talk about your future." *What*? I had only been in the role for 15 months. The expectation had been 2+ years. He said that the Petroleum Executive Leadership Team (PELT) had supported the recommendation that I be promoted to the VP of Engineering role and join the PELT. In my new assignment, I would be leading the small group of subject matter experts who supported the engineering and operations staff in the Petroleum division. I was shocked, humbled, honored, and overjoyed.

+++++++++++++++++++

This chapter has focused on my transition to a leadership role in a new company. We have seen the challenges of reestablishing your credibility. We have also seen how my prior experience in global operations prepared me for effectively leading the diverse teams across four locations around the world. We saw how the opportunities to develop others occurred in all the teams and across all levels of experience. We also saw how my diverse experience leading technical teams, operations teams, and financial/planning assignments was a strong foundation for stepping back into senior leadership roles. For those who may find themselves transitioning to a new company, you should consider (you will note that many of these points are similar to those to consider as you move into an executive role):

- Spending time early in the assignment to build connections to individual teams and members of your leadership team. Get to know your team members.
- Focusing on alignment across the organization on vision, values, and key deliverables.
- Understanding the drivers and decision style of any partners for your projects.
- Understanding and valuing the perspectives of organizations and individuals from different countries.
- Focusing your teams on delivering top performance to create value for the organization.
- When starting a new role, consider what you bring to the role from your past experience and what you can learn from the role to prepare for future roles.
- Stepping in to encourage your teams to gain alignment amongst themselves and other teams they interact with to deliver top-tier performance.

REFLECTION QUESTIONS:

- What have I done to connect with members of my team? What do I know about them personally? What drives them?

- Are our organization's vision, values, and critical success factors known across all teams? If so, are we aligned to deliver them? If not, what more can be done to improve the alignment?

- Have I considered the drivers and national culture of my business partners in the decision-making process for any projects awaiting approval?

- In recommending projects for approval, have I fully considered all possible outcomes, including failure, or am I biased to only the successful outcomes?

- How am I encouraging my teams to gain alignment with other teams to stop conflict and foster cooperation?

- Am I using each new assignment to learn new skills and prepare for future roles?

SUMMARY OF LEARNING POINTS – CHANGING COMPANIES

- Sometimes you have to take a step back to position yourself for future growth. Also, in looking at new opportunities and companies, remember that company culture is a key value for determining your fit in an organization. In some cases, it even trumps compensation.

- When stepping into a leadership role, a key to early success is building connections with your staff, your direct leader, and the other leaders in the organization you will be interfacing with. These connections are the foundation of effective engagement and support.

- REPEAT – Life can change suddenly. Pursue the things you love, both in your work and your life.

- As both an employee and a leader, company culture matters. Building relationships with each other and supporting each other in your time of need speaks volumes.

When you feel supported, your commitment and effort are strengthened.

- When dealing with multiple partners/team members, it is critical to make sure everyone feels that their input was heard and considered. Your job as a leader is to create the environment to allow full input and to facilitate the group to reach consensus on the path forward.

- As a leader, you will often interact with others with different backgrounds and/or from different regions of the world. To enhance your leadership capability, you have to have an awareness and consideration of their viewpoints, even if they are different from yours. Considering multiple viewpoints is a strength to be developed.

- As a leader of an organization, when evaluating a proposal or investment, don't let your bias/hope for a successful outcome cloud your judgment of the value of the project. And don't chase the hope for a positive outcome for too long. Sometimes, it takes a failure to teach you how to better evaluate opportunities and prepare for future projects.

- Building and broadening your skill set and experience can and will position you for future opportunities. Making sure others in leadership positions know your capabilities is also important. Don't sell yourself short, but at the same time, don't oversell your background. In the end, let your work speak for itself.

- REPEAT – As a senior leader, your words and actions matter. You set the standard for acceptable behavior. Set the standard high and live up to it.

- Training isn't always easy or fun. But it is important. Never skip your training. You never know when the skills you learn may be called into action. And they may even help save your life.

- As a senior leader, there is tremendous value in understanding your personality/behavior style, learning how to recognize other styles, and knowing how best to interact with other styles. Take time to do an assessment. A couple of my favorites are Merrill and Reid Social Styles and TTI Disc and Driving Forces.

- As a leader, take time to invest in your people. Their personal and professional growth is one measure of your own effectiveness as a leader. It can also be personally fulfilling to see their continued success.

- Misaligned objectives often result in subpar results. As a senior leader, your charge is to encourage teams to work together to reach an agreement on aligned objectives. This alignment is critical to position the organization for success. Get the teams working together, then step back and watch them exceed your expectations.

Chapter 10

Back to Senior Executive and Executive Leadership Team

After almost four years at BHP Billiton, I had moved from a senior manager role to a GM role and had just been promoted to be the VP of Engineering for the global petroleum portfolio. With this role, I would be returning to a senior executive role and joining the Petroleum Executive Leadership Team. After some pruning of my Career Tree when I switched companies, I had again grown in stature and was moving into a position to bear fruit for the organization, the technical staff, and myself.

This chapter will explore the challenges and opportunities that come as you become a member of an executive leadership team with joint accountability and responsibility for setting the direction of the company and ensuring delivery of results.

WELCOME

I was elated about my new role as VP of Engineering. Actually, this was the job I had interviewed for when I'd first considered changing companies. At that time, I had interviewed with several members of the Petroleum Leadership Team (PLT) but had been unsuccessful in landing the job. When the VP of HR called me with the decision, he said the PLT had been impressed by my background and wanted to stay in touch if future jobs came up. Who knew that six months later, I would be offered the senior manager role that brought me to the company?

Just before starting my VP role, I had the opportunity to address the summer interns at a Lunch and Learn seminar. At the end of the seminar, I spoke with the President of Production.

"Congratulations!" he said. "How long has it been since you first interviewed for the VP of Engineering role?"

"Just over four years," I replied.

"You've been very persistent in working your way up to the new role. You know, those four years you spent in other roles will be very useful in this new one. You now have a much broader network and relationships with the other company leaders and a much deeper understanding of the full portfolio of fields and projects."

I knew that both would be crucial to my success in the new role.

LEARNING POINT – In climbing your Career Tree, sometimes you have to go down a few branches to allow you to climb higher in the future. Persistence and focus are crucial to start your climb again. Use the time to expand your network and increase your knowledge of the company.

VISION AND CLARITY

The Central Engineering team was unique within the Petroleum division and BHP globally. We were a small team that housed the company-wide experts in facilities engineering, reservoir engineering, production engineering, operations, maintenance, and reserve reporting (SEC requirement mentioned in Chapter 8). Most of the staff were in their late-career stage with 20 to 30 years of experience and expertise, and had chosen to climb their Career Tree on the technical or functional route. They were often recognized as industry-wide experts as well. Each section of the team was led by a Chief Engineer, the highest technical role in the company.

The overall charge for the team was to be a resource for the technical and operations teams across the company. The team was facing a challenge because the VP role had been temporarily filled for the past year when the previous incumbent had been assigned to a special project and then an international role. During this period, the teams were, in a sense, coasting without clear guidance. My challenge was to reinvigorate the team members, engage with the PLT members and Asset leadership teams to align on areas of support, and strengthen the technical focus of the company.

As I had done with each new team I joined as the leader, I spent my first few days interacting with each member of the organization, learning about their backgrounds, areas of expertise, work in progress, and any concerns they may have. After a couple of weeks, I called the entire group together and outlined the five key focus areas I had gleaned from my discussions with all the team members. They were:

- Set the standard for quality technical work
- Assess technical work being done in the assets against the technical standards
- Provide technical support/advice to the assets on complex issues
- Develop the technical capabilities and skills across all experience levels in the organization (early, mid, and late)
- Compile and submit the final reserve report to the SEC (corporate deliverable)

The charge for our Central Engineering team was to engage with staff and leaders across the assets to build relationships and deliver on our top focus areas. We needed to work hard on delivering value for the assets so that we would be seen as more than just an overhead cost. After the group discussion, the team embraced the key deliverables and accepted the task of engaging across the organization.

LEARNING POINT – A key deliverable for a senior leader is providing clarity and focus on critical success factors for the organization and gaining alignment and commitment for delivering outstanding results. This is not something you can delegate down the line. Own it and make it happen.

PEER FEEDBACK

After setting the course for my team, I had to take the same actions I had charged them with, particularly engaging my peers to get feedback on their areas of concern within their organizations and on how the Central Engineering organization was performing. Generally, the feedback was good. However, in discussions with one of the GMs, I gave him some feedback that my teams felt his organization was excluding them from technical problems where they could add valuable input and advice. He countered that his teams felt that interacting with Central Engineering was like talking to a black hole: inquiries go in, but nothing comes out. Rather than react, I asked for some examples. It seemed that there had been instances where the asset team had asked for input for a question that needed addressing within a week or two, but didn't hear back from the CE team for over a month. I thanked the GM for the feedback and promised to address it with my team.

At our next monthly CE All Hands meeting, I brought up the topic that the assets felt CE was a "black hole." The immediate reaction from the team was defensive and one of disbelief. I gave the example that if a team asked for guidance within a week and we took a month, then we were a black hole. I also challenged them to leverage their own position on their Career Tree as a technical expert. With 20 to 30 years of experience, they probably had an 80% solution to the inquiry from the asset on the top of their head or within a day or two. I recommended that the approach be to give the early guidance to the assets to point them in the right direction, and then state that we would give more detailed guidance within the next two weeks as we evaluated the issue in more detail. The teams appreciated the recognition of their expertise and accepted the proposed approach to the assets. Over the next few months, the interactions between the asset teams and Central Engineering became more frequent and collaborative. The "black hole" was gone, and a bridge had been put in its place.

LEARNING POINT – Feedback (both positive and negative) is a gift. As a senior leader, you should be seeking frequent feedback on how you and your teams are doing, especially if you are in a service role. But to make feedback even more valuable, you have to reflect, act, and respond to the input from others.

HELPING OTHERS GROW – THE CAREER TREE IS BORN

Earlier in this chapter, I pointed out that one of the five critical success factors for Central Engineering was to "Develop the technical capabilities and skills across all experience levels in the organization (early, mid, late)." I truly believed this and felt that I had a major role in making this happen. In fact, one of my direct accountabilities was the development of our 300+ engineering staff in the company. I wanted to make sure that I engaged with each one on a frequent and periodic basis. I set a personal goal to meet with each engineer at least twice per year, including those in Pakistan, Trinidad and Tobago, and Australia.

One of the ways I started interacting with the engineers was by having breakfast sessions with different groups. With most of the engineers based in Houston, I started having weekly breakfast sessions for small groups of 12 to 15. In this setting, I could share some insights from my perspective, take questions, and give some career advice. I was doing this across all experience levels of the organization.

After a couple of months, I found myself giving different guidance to different groups of engineers based on their experience level. Thinking back to the career maps I had generated in Brunei (see Chapter 8), I started introducing the concept of the Career Tree into these discussions. The analogy really helped me focus my guidance to the specific point of where people were in their careers. For the junior staff, we spoke quite a lot about building core skills to grow a strong trunk for future success. At the same time, the Career Tree analogy helped me talk to them about opportunities they could and should consider as they climbed higher. It was rewarding to see these early-career individuals pick up the theme of getting good at their craft while still keeping in mind the options and opportunities for 5 to 10 years down the road.

One of the most surprising outcomes was with the late-career individuals. Many of them entered the breakfast sessions with a mindset that they had plateaued, and the remainder of their career would be spent just doing the same thing again and again. I introduced the concept of the Career Tree to them and acknowledged that they (like me) were in the late career phase. I also introduced the concept that this was the time to grow in stature and bear fruit, not wither away. I challenged them to think of how they might bear fruit. I was greatly encouraged to see several step up to partner with early and mid-career individuals, serving as a mentor (both on technical and personal skills).

I came to relish my weekly breakfast. I never knew what questions that the group might ask. They kept me on my toes. And I like to think that I helped them in defining the path of climbing their own Career Tree.

LEARNING POINT – As a senior leader, taking time to invest in others to help them navigate their path to success as they climb their Career Tree is a rewarding investment. You likely had someone to help and guide you. Be that leader and guide to someone else.

FINDING YOUR VOICE – DON'T BE SILENT

One of the responsibilities of the VP of Engineering role was as a member of the Petroleum Leadership Team. It was a fairly large team with 10 people, including the President and the leaders representing the line organizations, central technical functions, and support organizations. Our charge was to set the direction of the Petroleum division, ensure alignment with the global BHP Billiton organization, and deliver the promised performance.

It wasn't my first time on an executive leadership team. That had been in Brunei, which was smaller, with only five people. We also had a few more constraints on our areas of focus and ways of working with oversight from both Shell and the Bruneian government. That experience was a good foundation from which to grow, but the BHP Billiton role had even greater expectations.

I spent my first few months as a part of the PLT in the VP role observing the dynamics of the group and doing short report-outs on the key technical projects the Central Engineering team was working on in support of the asset teams. As I became more comfortable in the role and with the PLT ways of working, I would occasionally offer more input but was still one of the less vocal members of the team. I could say that part of that fits with the Analytical Social style that was secondary in my Merrill and Reid profile.

During my first performance review in the VP role, the President of Petroleum gave me some challenging feedback. He said that I had more value to add to the PLT beyond just my technical expertise and focus on staff development. He said that as important decisions were being discussed, he wanted to hear my voice. Now the tough message – he said he didn't add me to the team just to fill a seat or to echo the opinions of others. He wanted my unique perspective and voice. While I generally portrayed characteristics of an extrovert, I still had quite a bit of the HS nerd introvert in me. I liked to reflect on a situation and then respond accordingly. It was tough (and scary) for me to respond immediately. I shared that with my boss. He understood but still emphasized that my voice needed to be heard. This became an area of personal focus. I would need to increase my effectiveness in this area to continue to grow in stature as a senior leader.

LEARNING POINT – Many senior leaders get to that position of stature based on their experience and expertise in a particular functional area, be it engineering, project management, HR, finance, etc. But being an effective member of an executive leadership team demands more. You have to find your unique voice to add to ELT discussions. And don't be afraid to use it.

TOUGH DECISIONS I (AND USING MY VOICE)

As I mentioned previously in this chapter, one of the focus areas of the Central Engineering team was to provide technical assurance of the operations assets. One afternoon, one of my chiefs stopped by my desk with an urgent issue. We stepped into one of the huddle rooms to discuss further. (We had recently moved into a new building with an open concept with everyone, including the Petroleum Leadership Team members, having only desks out in the open bullpen.) The chief informed me that a major project was underperforming to the point that we needed to update the President of Petroleum. The issue was of such magnitude that it would also need to be reported to the BHP executive team. We took some time that afternoon for me to understand the magnitude of the issue.

I requested a meeting with the President for the next day for the two of us to review the issue with him. At the meeting, the chief explained the issue, outlining the shortfall in performance and what it meant for that segment of the business. The President was shocked at first. He asked why this was the first he was hearing about the magnitude of the issue and what was being done to possibly offset part of the negative impact. I could also see him getting angry. Once again, I thought it might be another "shoot the messenger" event.

At this point, I realized I had made a big error in my haste to schedule the meeting. I had bypassed the VP of that business segment and gone straight to the President. In hindsight, it would have been better to engage the VP with the concerns and then have him involved in disclosing the information to the President. The VP would have been in a much better position to address the questions the President was asking, as I and the chief only had information at a high level and could not speak to specific activities within the asset teams. As we could not give the President specifics, I closed the meeting and assured him we would engage with the VP and asset teams to bring him a more complete picture of options to reduce the impact of the underperformance.

On a personal note, this cooled my relationship with the President for the next several months. The negative news had had an impact on his standing with the global leaders and the board. I think he still felt that I shared some of the responsibility for the poor performance and lack of transparency in communication. Personally, I vowed to improve my engagement with the other members of the PLT, including the President, with emphasis on identifying challenges, highlighting areas needing support from Central Engineering, and aligning positions on performance and communication.

REPEAT LEARNING POINT – When delivering a tough message, expect resistance. Be calm and present your case professionally and purposefully. Engaging with others without becoming overly emotional or loud will give you a better chance at gaining alignment.

LEARNING POINT – When communicating a tough message to senior leaders, be sure that you have linked with other affected parties so that you are aligned on the problem and also options to address the issue at hand. Lack of alignment and transparency only makes a problem worse.

EXTENDING MY IMPACT

While the Engineering function and Central Engineering advisory team were well-positioned in the Petroleum division, these groups were not given as much emphasis and support in other parts of the global company. At our annual conference of senior leaders, I met some colleagues who ran technical teams or mines across the globe. They showed interest in how my team was set up. We had some initial discussions on how the concept could be applied within their organizations to bring greater emphasis to the Engineering discipline.

One of the individuals I met was the Head of Geoscience for the mining sector of BHP. She offered to connect me with some of the engineering managers at the larger mines around the world. Working with my Chief Facilities Engineer, we formed a working group with the Engineering Managers at key mines in South America and Australia. I volunteered to serve as the chair of this working group, even though it meant additional responsibilities. It also meant some early starts and late nights to connect with the teams around the world.

The early meetings of this Global Working Group focused on the role the facilities engineers played in Petroleum (primarily overseeing mechanical equipment at producing fields), which was very similar to the engineering staff in the Mining sector of the company. We also reviewed how the Central Engineering teams supported the deployed engineers in the assets by setting the standards for good work, assessing technical work against the standards, providing expert technical advice on complex problems, and developing the technical capabilities of the engineering staff. These same activities were being done for the geoscience staff in the Mining sector, but only on a limited and local basis for engineering staff.

Working with key engineering leaders in both sectors, we collectively identified major areas of focus to enhance the engineering capabilities in the Mining sector. One key learning was not to try to duplicate the Petroleum methodology and overlay into Mining. Instead, the best and most effective approach was found to be to capture the key concept and intent of each process and then fit those to the Mining ways of working. That didn't mean we didn't directly apply Petroleum techniques where processes were absent in Mining, but those were few.

Another critical success factor was finding the right leader at the major sites to be a change agent and champion for the new ways of working. There were a few individuals who stood out. Many of them had already been identified by the Chief Geologist for Mining and assigned to the Global Working Group. These individuals provided great insight into the activities within Mining and how best to "tweak" the Petroleum processes for buy-in and ownership within Mining. (As an aside, during this period in the company, the Mining sector of BHP was often reluctant to accept input or recommendations from Petroleum, so we were facing an uphill climb in making wholesale changes based on a Petroleum way of working.)

These change agents in Mining were often not senior leaders but instead mid-level managers with a passion for improving their local site's performance. To be effective, they had to work upwards in convincing their senior manager of the case for action, and in some instances, investment in equipment to facilitate improvement. The change agent also had to work down the organization chart to the field operations teams to implement new standards and ways of working. It took a while to gain traction, but in the end, the work by the engineering teams in Mining was seen as value added and once again a good career path for growing and climbing one's Career Tree. This was exciting to see.

LEARNING POINT – As a senior leader, look for those opportunities to help others. But don't approach those interactions with the attitude of "I am right, just do it my way." Instead, to see real change that sticks, approach the interaction through engagement, learning how best to help other groups improve.

REPEAT LEARNING POINT – Helping others improve and succeed isn't a sign of weakness. In fact, it is a sign of strength.

TOUGH DECISIONS II AND WINDING DOWN

After several years in the VP role, the Petroleum organization was selling its position in the US onshore sector. As a consequence, the remaining groups would be restructuring to streamline support for the conventional offshore operations around the world in the US, Australia, and Trinidad and Tobago, along with the recent successful entry to deepwater exploration in Mexico. After a long tenure, the question put to me by the President of Petroleum and the PLT was: "What should the Central Engineering organization look like in the new design and what should be its remit?" Similar questions were asked of my colleague, who was the VP of Geoscience. In addition to being colleagues, we had become good friends during our time on the PLT, often working closely together to tackle technical challenges in an integrated approach, including both geoscience and engineering perspectives. He had been with BHP for most of his career, while I had been with them for over 7 years now.

To address the organizational design challenge presented to us, we decided to work together on a proposed recommendation. During the sales process for the US onshore business, we had started discussions about what a new organization would look like. One common theme was that we should really combine our organizations, even if it meant eliminating one of our jobs. Like my experience in the speech writing in Chapter 5, we each made an initial draft of the remit and design of the combined group. Interestingly, they were very similar. Together, we had incorporated elements from each group that we considered strengths. These included setting standards, assessing performance, providing technical support to the asset teams, defining and documenting ways of working, and developing technical staff.

With a few tweaks to fully align our individual designs, we were ready to present our joint recommendation to the PLT. We had included a recommended list of candidates for the chief roles but had not included recommendations for the VP role. In a one-on-one discussion with my boss, he asked me for my thoughts on qualified candidates for the new combined VP role we had recommended. I expressed my interest in the role and also gave a short list of other names, some who were ready now and some who could do the role with support while they were still growing in their senior leadership skills. Many of the names were also individuals I had coached and mentored (and even supervised) during my time at BHP. With general support from the PLT, my VP of Geoscience colleague and I worked on finalizing the team design with a build-out of all the positions needed and recommendations on individuals to fill each role.

The two of us were also charged with reviewing the proposed asset team designs. While some of the staff would be transitioning to the buyers of the US onshore properties, overall, the new organization would require fewer staff than currently with the company. As the "owners" of staff assessments and development, my geoscience colleague and I would play a major role in final recommendations for staff assignments. Talk about a tough role. Over the past four years in my VP of Engineering role, I had come to know all 300+ engineers individually.

The PLT decided to do a series of placement meetings. The first pass was to name the individuals filling the various leadership roles. This was done by the PLT itself and included the GM, chiefs, and manager roles across all departments. The next step was to conduct a series of similar sessions for the various departments with the named managers participating. Prior to these sessions, I had a meeting with the President. I remember that it was my birthday that day. We started off talking about the organization design overall and then the combined geoscience/engineering central team. He said he would "cut to the chase" and said that neither my colleague nor I had been chosen to lead the new organization. Bummer. This was not the birthday present I was hoping for.

He disclosed the successful candidate. It had been one of the names I had proposed as a good candidate. I was happy for the individual as she had worked for me in a couple of assignments, where I had coached her on her leadership development, like all my direct reports. After my initial shock and disappointment, I realized that it was time to step back and let someone else continue climbing their own Career Tree.

LEARNING POINT – As a senior leader, you will face some tough choices, particularly around personnel assignments, including your own future. In working through the options and recommendations, stay committed to your values and do what is right for the individual and the organization.

Now, I had a personal choice – I could "check out" since I was no longer going to be the leader in the new organization, or I could stay committed to seeing the new organization get up and running. For me, it wasn't a hard choice. I had never walked away before.

With the new leadership positions filled, I spent my last few months with BHP ensuring that the new organization design and ways of working were well known by the incoming leaders. I also worked to create a thorough handover with the new VP of Technical Services to help set her up for success. I did a series of visits to the Petroleum teams in Trinidad and Australia to encourage the technical staff in those locations to stay focused on delivering their commitments even during the transition period of the new organization. Finally, I visited the engineering teams of the major mines in South America and Southern Australia, encouraging them to stay focused on the key areas being advanced by the Global Engineering Working Group. With these final engagements, I was ready to step away. Over the past 8+ years with BHP, I had continued to grow in stature and bear fruit in helping so many grow their own skills.

LEARNING POINT – When your role is no longer there, don't check out and lose interest. See it through to the end and exit with grace.

+++++++++++++++++++

This chapter has focused on my return to a senior executive role and being a part of an executive leadership team with shared accountability for the overall success of the organization. We have seen again the emphasis and value of building early connections with a team and working partners. We have also seen the impact of providing clarity on the organization's vision, direction, and responding to feedback in a positive manner. Even as I returned to a senior leader position, we have seen that no leadership level is too high to invest in helping others grow in their careers. We have seen how senior leaders must make tough decisions regarding performance and personnel. Finally, we have seen the value in finding your voice, making it heard, and extending your impact. For those who may find themselves in a senior leadership role and part of the executive team, you should consider (again, note the similarity to considerations of executive roles):

- Spending time early in the assignment to build connections to individual teams and members of your leadership team. Get to know your team members.
- Likewise, spending time building connections with your fellow executive team members and understanding how your individual organizations interact and support one another
- Building clarity on organizational purpose, vision, values, and key deliverables.
- Dedicating time to helping staff at all levels continue their development and career growth.
- Volunteering to be a mentor to an emerging leader.
- Finding your voice and using it to further discussions, not just being an echo.

- Stepping up to make tough decisions when required. Don't abdicate.

REFLECTION QUESTIONS:

- What have I done to connect with members of my team? What do I know about them personally? What drives them?
- How am I connecting my organization with other segments of the business?
- Are our organization's Purpose, Vision, Values, and Critical Success Factors known across all teams? If so, are we aligned to deliver them? If not, what more can be done to improve the alignment?
- How am I helping emerging leaders develop their skills for future leadership roles? Who am I mentoring?
- How am I using my voice on the executive leadership team? Am I staying silent? If so, why? Am I just being an echo chamber of others? What is my unique position, and how am I expressing it to my ELT team members?
- Am I stepping up to make the tough decisions in my organization or am I allowing others to do so for me?

SUMMARY OF LEARNING POINTS – RETURN TO SENIOR EXECUTIVE AND EXECUTIVE LEADERSHIP TEAM

- In climbing your Career Tree, sometimes you have to go down a few branches to allow you to climb higher in the future. Persistence and focus are crucial to start your climb again. Use the time to expand your network and increase your knowledge of the company.
- A key deliverable for a senior leader is providing clarity and focus on critical success factors for the organization and

gaining alignment and commitment for delivering outstanding results. This is not something you can delegate down the line. Own it and make it happen.

- Feedback (both positive and negative) is a gift. As a senior leader, you should be seeking frequent feedback on how you and your teams are doing, especially if you are in a service role. But to make feedback even more valuable, you have to reflect, act, and respond to the input from others.

- As a senior leader, taking time to invest in others to help them navigate their path to success as they climb their Career Tree is a rewarding investment. You likely had someone to help and guide you. Be that leader and guide to someone else.

- Many senior leaders get to that position of stature based on their experience and expertise in a particular functional area, be it engineering, project management, HR, finance, etc. But being an effective member of an executive leadership team demands more. You have to find your unique voice to add to ELT discussions. And don't be afraid to use it.

- REPEAT – When delivering a tough message, expect resistance. Be calm and present your case professionally and purposefully. Engaging with others without becoming overly emotional or loud will give you a better chance at gaining alignment.

- When communicating a tough message to senior leaders, be sure that you have linked with other affected parties so that you are aligned on the problem and also options to address the issue at hand. Lack of alignment and transparency only makes a problem worse.

- As a senior leader, look for those opportunities to help others. But don't approach those interactions with the attitude of "I am right, just do it my way." Instead, to see real change that sticks, approach the interaction through engagement, learning how best to help other groups improve.
- REPEAT – Helping others improve and succeed isn't a sign of weakness. In fact, it is a sign of strength.
- As a senior leader, you will face some tough choices, particularly around personnel assignments, including your own future. In working through the options and recommendations, stay committed to your values and do what is right for the individual and the organization.
- When your role is no longer there, don't check out and lose interest. See it through to the end and exit with grace.

Chapter 11

(Semi) Retirement – Stepping Back and Serving Others by Giving Back

After over 36 years in the oil and gas industry, I had now retired for the 2nd time. I didn't really want to work full-time again, but at the same time, I wasn't ready to play golf every day. The real question was, "What am I going to do with the rest of my life?"

This chapter will explore the challenges and opportunities that come as you have reached the point in your Career Tree where you have stopped climbing and are moving into helping others define, grow, and climb their own Career Tree. It's time to give back.

RETIRED (AGAIN)

At my retirement party (2nd time around), I was humbled by the outpouring of support and love shown by my work colleagues, from the junior engineers to my fellow PLT members. It was great to have my wife there. She had been with me from the beginning in New Orleans, back and forth between Houston and New Orleans, overseas to Brunei, and back again without a defined future path. Both of our adult children flew in to attend the event. They had been a part of this journey as well, and I was so grateful to have them share in the celebration.

Many people at the event were asking me what was next. The immediate answer was easy. We were headed to North Carolina the next day to see my daughter receive her PhD degree. I was so proud of her. The longer-term answer was more difficult. I had spent over 36 years growing and climbing my Career Tree. In some ways, I had fallen into the trap of estimating my value to society by my job. While I enjoyed some hobbies of reading, gardening, golfing, and bicycling, I didn't see myself doing that every day for however long I might live. In discussions with my wife after we knew the 2nd retirement was coming, she gave me some great advice. She said I needed to find something to do as I couldn't sit around the house all day watching sports, talk shows (and/or game shows/soap operas), and disrupting her routines.

That got me thinking about what I wanted this next phase to be. I came across the book *Don't Retire, Rewire!* by Jeri Sedlar and Rick Miners. Reading through the chapters really helped me identify the activities that brought me fulfillment and joy, which included lifelong learning, making a difference, mentoring others, and problem-solving. Ok, so what could I do with what I just learned?

LEARNING POINT – Retirement doesn't mean checking out and parking on the sidelines of life. Find the activities that bring you joy and reframe your "spare" time to engage in the things that fulfill you.

PROFESSOR AND INTERN (AT THE SAME TIME)

Just as I was working through the activities that I enjoyed, two opportunities opened that got me started on my active retirement path. Interestingly, they were alike and different at the same time. The common path was that they each gave me an opportunity to make a difference by helping others and solving problems. They were different in how each activity might be viewed by others.

The first opportunity was with my alma mater, Mississippi State University (MSU). I had been serving on the Advisory Board for the Petroleum Engineering program in the Swalm School of Chemical Engineering. In our initial ABET accreditation review, the primary feedback was strengthening the Capstone senior design class. When the Director of the department shared the results in our fall advisory board meeting, my interest was piqued. I was a couple of months from retirement and thought this might be fun. After the meeting, I spoke to the Director and offered my services to help teach the capstone class. My intent was to use my 36+ years of experience in the industry, my Professional Engineering license, and my last 4.5 years as VP of Engineering to bring real-world projects to the class for the students to work. This would give them experience working on projects and using software that they would encounter as petroleum engineers in the industry. I wanted to help prepare them for the workforce on day one of growing their own Career Tree. Now in 2026, I am in my 8th year of teaching the class with my friend and colleague, Dr. Mohammad Heshmati. It truly has been a joy. I don't even mind the 4+ hour drive each month to engage with the students for their presentations. My only disappointment has been that I didn't make better use of my negotiating skills, as I teach the class as a volunteer Adjunct Professor.

The second opportunity came from a nonprofit board position. From my GM and VP roles at BHP, I had been a board member for a nonprofit that the company supported. As my retirement was announced, I spoke to the Executive Director about replacing me on the board because I would no longer be in a corporate role and could not bring in corporate support. She understood the situation and thanked me for my past service, but she didn't want to lose my input to the leadership of the organization. As we talked further, we came up with a unique proposal. When the new year started, I would become the unpaid INTERN (see the Robert DeNiro movie) supporting the leadership of the nonprofit. (Again, my negotiating skills failed me on my pay package – HA.) My emphasis would be to help them review their work processes, looking for ways to streamline operations and interactions between groups, plus building their annual budget and planning processes. It had been several years since I had done either. It was fun to refresh the skills and apply them to a group that could use the help.

Both of these opportunities gave me a chance to use skills I had developed during my career to help others. While I may not be climbing higher in my Career Tree, I was definitely bearing fruit by serving others. I was getting personal satisfaction, and I was staying out of my wife's hair (and hopefully out of trouble).

LEARNING POINT – As you reach the top of your Career Tree, continue "bearing fruit" by looking for opportunities to use your experience, skills, and expertise to help others.

You, too, can find satisfaction and fulfillment as you see others improve.

BACK TO NEW ORLEANS AND UNEXPECTED OPPORTUNITIES

When I started my VP role, my wife and I started discussions on where we wanted to live in retirement. We had considered a couple of locations and finally landed on returning to New Orleans, where I had first planted the seed of my Career Tree and where we first lived after getting married. We even knew exactly where we wanted to live, back in the Lakeview neighborhood in New Orleans. We called our plan to return to NOLA our "2020 Plan." We actually found the perfect house within our desired area in 2016. Although four years before our "planned" date, we bought the house and rented it to another family. After my retirement, we hired a local architect and made the renovations to the house that we had envisioned. By the end of 2019, the house was ready to move in. We sold our house in Houston and moved ourselves and two cats to New Orleans in mid-January. Who knew that the city would shut down due to the COVID pandemic just 6 weeks after we got settled? We had met our "2020 Plan" if maybe 9 or 10 months earlier than originally planned. We were glad to be in our house, and with the shutdown, we spent much of the time outside exploring the nearby City Park. We even learned a new sport of disc golf courtesy of our son, who spent the last half of his last semester at Georgia Tech University in our newly renovated upstairs living space. It was a great way to get some exercise and have fun while the city was shut down. I'm not sure my disc golf handicap ever got as low as my golf handicap, but the occasional great shot was all the encouragement needed to go back out again.

With the move to New Orleans, I still had my MSU teaching responsibilities but had completed my "Internship" at the Houston nonprofit. That internship led to the opportunity to do the same type of work with the nonprofit affiliate location in New Orleans. Once meeting restrictions had been lifted, I met with the New Orleans Executive Director and CFO and talked about the work I had done in Houston and where I might be able to help in New Orleans. After our initial meeting, we were all eager to start working together. They were looking for some more strategic support, and I was looking for another internship. YAY. But my negotiating skills still sucked as I was still unpaid. HA. But I readily accepted the opportunity for the chance to apply my skills to help another group. Over the next couple of years, I worked with this New Orleans affiliate and a couple of other nonprofits, focusing on mapping their strategic plan and improving their operational performance.

I was enjoying the nonprofit work but was still a little bored. A chance encounter with a colleague from Shell changed all that. At a Shell retiree lunch, we ran into each other and talked about what each of us was doing. I talked about my work with nonprofits and helping define their strategic plans and improve operational performance. My colleague said he had purchased the local franchise of The Alternative Board (TAB), which coaches business owners to improve their businesses. My colleague said that what I was doing with nonprofits, he was doing for small business owners in the Greater New Orleans region. In addition to one-on-one coaching, in the TAB model, the business owners came together once a month in a "board" meeting, serving as board members to help each other address issues and opportunities.

My colleague said the engagements with local business owners built on our experiences as executives at Shell, plus additional skills in coaching and board facilitation. The concept sounded very interesting, and I agreed to go through the formal training for my coaching certification. I was excited about this opportunity.

LEARNING POINT – Again, as you reach the top of your Career Tree and are looking for the next chance to apply your skills, maintain and grow your network. Keep your eyes, ears, and connections open and active, as you never know where your next and best opportunity will come from.

GROWING AS AN EFFECTIVE COACH (AND OWNER)

After completing my coaching training, I now had to recruit my members for coaching and my own boards. *What*? While I enjoyed interacting with others, I was no salesman. I loved to talk and learn about people, but asking them to do business with me? One of the tools we used with our TAB clients was a DISC and Driving Forces assessment by TTI Success Insights. DISC focuses on "how" a person behaves, while the Driving Forces focuses on the motivators of "why" a person behaves. My DISC profile showed that I was more Reflective/Modest (D), Outgoing/Poised (I), Steady/Patient (S) [My wife does not agree with the Patient label], and Precise/Accurate (C). The Driving Forces said my motivators were Selflessness and Altruism – focused on helping others, along with Intellectual approach and Collaboration. Interestingly, these Driving Forces motivators closely aligned with my own analysis from the Don't Retire, Rewire book. Who knows, maybe this TAB approach was onto something.

With my own DISC assessment and coaching certification in hand, I decided to start slowly in building my clientele, mainly attending local Chamber of Commerce networking events. After a couple of months, I was starting to get the hang of making my pitch but was still struggling to sign clients. I ended my first year with only one person, not enough for a board meeting, so we did coaching only. I am thankful she agreed to sign up with me, as the interactions in our coaching sessions gave me confidence in my ability to fulfill the role of coach. Now the push was to sign more clients and get the critical mass for a board.

After my first year, my Shell colleague asked if I would like to be a partner in the business. This was exciting and scary at the same time. I had spent my career working in corporations. Even though I had led several business segments and run them like my own business, I had never actually been the owner. Now was the time to go forward with confidence or step back. I decided to jump in and became a partner in the business. Now that I had a financial stake in the performance of the franchise, my drive to add clients and get a board started was enhanced. Within six months of agreeing to become a partner in the business, I had my first full board of business owners up and running. Most were small business owners with 2 to 15 employees. I also had a few clients who were only getting monthly coaching as a part of their leadership development at larger companies. I was up and running and having fun.

I was making progress in building my boards of business owners, but I had also said I didn't want another full-time job after "retiring" twice before. I set a personal limit of two boards and 20 total clients (including those with coaching only). I had estimated that this level of coaching and board meetings would take me less than 50% of a full-time schedule each month. This would still allow me to teach at Mississippi State University and have some personal time. Over the next few months, I continued to add new members to my board, primarily through contacts at Chamber events. As I attended more Chamber activities, I was invited to become an Ambassador for the New Orleans Chamber. As an Ambassador, I got to advocate for the value of the Chamber to its members and help recruit new members. This was an easy job as I could see the results for my own business.

After almost a year and a half as a partner, and with my ongoing success in attracting clients, I was making steady progress in reaching my limit of 20 clients. I had filled a full board with 8 members, plus I had another 5 members doing coaching only, and was about to start a series of strategy workshops for a local nonprofit. During one of our board meetings, a member said that the sessions were really "business therapy" for business owners. I fully agreed. I felt that I was making a difference for my members. As a result, I was becoming more enthusiastic about the business and spending more time on the coaching activities.

At this point, I had two critical conversations. The first was with my real boss, my wife, who said I wasn't following my own advice to my clients. I was starting each month trying to schedule the client interactions for that month. She said I needed to get more structured in my schedule to allow the time for my teaching, for myself, and for us as a couple to do things together. I said YES, MA'AM, and promptly started setting regular schedules for all my TAB events and not attending every single Chamber event. We even scheduled vacation time for us to be away for almost three weeks to visit the Galapagos Islands and Machu Picchu. What a fantastic trip, even if my fear of drowning made me a little hesitant during the snorkeling outings. It was a once-in-a-lifetime event with my best friend and companion. We got to celebrate our belated 40th anniversary and our 41st anniversary as a part of the trip. And I came back to find the structure of meetings had held and made my weekly and monthly planning much easier. I guess the old adage of "Physician, heal thyself" was true. Maybe mine should have been "Coach, follow your own advice."

The second conversation was with my business partner. He said that he and his wife had decided to accelerate their move out of the New Orleans area to another state where they had a second home. He asked if I would like to buy a portion of his stake in the business and become the majority owner. While we had previously discussed the possibility, the potential timing had been a year or so later. I thought about it, prayed, and talked to my wife. In the end, it was an easy decision. I loved interacting with my business owner clients and helping them improve their businesses in ways that were changing their lives. Together, my business partner and I had also started bringing on additional coaches and board facilitators, plus a strategy workshop facilitator, to expand our offerings to more business owners. And as the majority owner, I could help shape the impact TAB could have across the entire Greater New Orleans area. In the end, it was an easy decision.

LEARNING POINT – As opportunities present themselves, be sure to test them against your drivers and motivators. As you do, you can very well find activities and endeavors that bring your fulfillment even as you reach the top of your Career Tree. Use this time to start helping others in their own career path.

Now, when someone asks what I do, I say, besides being a loving husband and father, I am the Owner of TAB New Orleans, an Adjunct Professor of Petroleum Engineering at Mississippi State University, a faithful member and deacon at First Baptist Church New Orleans, and sometimes a decent golf player. And, *fully content* that I have climbed my Career Tree to the level I wanted and have indeed grown in stature and borne fruit in helping others on their own career path.

+++++++++++++++++++

This chapter has focused on my transition from senior executive and active member of an executive leadership team to (semi) retirement. We have seen the challenge of figuring out your path forward as you move from active work to unstructured and ample time. We saw how reflecting on what motivates you and brings you contentment and joy can unlock opportunities for you to give back and help others in the apex of your career journey. For those who may find themselves at this phase of exiting full-time work, you should consider:

- Evaluating your drivers and motivators for activities that bring you fulfillment.
- Maintaining and growing your professional and personal networks. You never know which connection may lead to

that opportunity that is the best fit for your next phase of life (and) work.

- Finding the right balance point for you on work, family, and personal time and commitments. When the balance is right, everyone (and especially you) can be happy.
- Giving back where you can. Tell your story. Let others learn from your life experiences.

REFLECTION QUESTIONS:

- Do I know what motivates me to get up each day and go out in life?
- Am I maintaining my network connections? Maybe even more importantly, am I growing my connections (personal and professional)?
- What activities am I trying to see if they align with my motivators and bring me fulfillment in where I spend my time?
- How am I helping others in this period where I can give back?

SUMMARY OF LEARNING POINTS – (SEMI) RETIREMENT – STEPPING BACK & SERVING OTHERS BY GIVING BACK

- Retirement doesn't mean checking out and parking on the sidelines of life. Find the activities that bring you joy and reframe your "spare" time to engage in the things that fulfill you.
- As you reach the top of your Career Tree, continue "bearing fruit" by looking for opportunities to use your experience,

skills, and expertise to help others. You, too, can find satisfaction and fulfillment as you see others improve.

- Again, as you reach the top of your Career Tree and are looking for the next chance to apply your skills, maintain and grow your network. Keep your eyes, ears, and connections open and active, as you never know where your next and best opportunity will come from.
- As opportunities present themselves, be sure to test them against your drivers and motivators. As you do, you can very well find activities and endeavors that bring your fulfillment even as you reach the top of your Career Tree. Use this time to start helping others in their own career path.

Chapter 12

Navigating the Challenges of Leadership Transitions

As I climbed my Career Tree from individual contributor roles up through multiple levels of leadership to senior executive roles, I experienced challenges in transition from one level to another. In this chapter, I will share my observations and learnings to help the readers understand the change in roles and responsibilities and the change in business timeline focus at the different levels as they make these same transitions. Many of these points have been shared in previous chapters as I went through the leadership transitions myself. I have compiled them in this single chapter as a summary and reference guide for the readers. Use them to reflect as you make a specific transition and what to consider for future roles.

FIRST SUPERVISION – FROM INDIVIDUAL CONTRIBUTOR TO SUPERVISOR

The transition from an individual contributor to a first leadership/supervisor role can bring unique challenges. The primary responsibility as a supervisor is no longer doing the work yourself, but instead ensuring quality work is being done by the other team members. You must now guide and review the work of the other team members. Your job isn't to do their work for them, nor is it to double-check their work. But you have to have enough functional knowledge to know quality work and know the scope of work that needs to be done.

The timeframe for your business focus shifts from day-to-day activities and tasks to monthly, quarterly, and yearly milestones. Your focus is to ensure work progresses and moves towards deliverable deadlines in a timely manner without stressing/overworking your team.

LEARNING POINT – As a supervisor, your success is dependent on the success of the individual team members. Knowing their strengths and areas for improvement, and building a sense of collective ownership, are foundations for success. Your business timeframe focus shifts from daily/weekly activities to monthly/quarterly/yearly work scope and planning to ensure timely delivery of work product without stressing the team.

SUPERVISOR TO MANAGER

While the move from individual contributor to supervisor has the challenge of guiding and reviewing the technical work of others, the move from supervisor to manager comes with the added challenges of setting direction and coordinating with other groups. The manager role also comes with increased accountability for delivering timely results (budgets and deadlines). You also move from managing individuals to managing other leaders. As a result, you are a step removed from the daily activities.

Your timeframe for business focus shifts from monthly/quarterly to a longer perspective. Your focus is on quarterly/yearly targets and goals and providing input and perspective on 2-year and 5-year strategic objectives.

LEARNING POINT – The move to a manager role means growing new skills beyond your core functional skills. You have to become adept at interfacing with other leaders, coordinating with other teams, aligning multiple teams to deliver results, and working through others to get the results you want. You can no longer rely on just your own personal technical capabilities. You will also play a more active role in setting strategic objectives and annual targets.

MANAGER TO EXECUTIVE

The move to an executive role brings expanded responsibilities and deliverables. At this level, you will likely have accountability for the overall performance of your division, including financial Profit & Loss (P&L). While daily and monthly performance are still vital to help ensure delivery for the year, your focus is on making sure your group/division is on the path to delivering its share for the whole company. You also hold the responsibility for defining the culture of your larger organization. This includes alignment on goals, direction, staff development, and vision. You will also play a larger role in setting direction for the company.

Your timeframe for business focus continues to shift to longer-term horizons. Yes, you have accountability for annual performance. But probably more importantly, you need to be looking 3 to 5 years ahead to position your organization for continued success.

LEARNING POINT – As an executive, your accountability expands beyond just annual goals and targets. You now play a key role in setting the vision for your organization and gaining alignment on direction and deliverables. You need to be looking 3 to 5 years ahead to position your organization for continued success. You have moved into the position where your words and actions set the tone for the group and have a strong influence on performance. Be clear, concise, and encouraging.

EXECUTIVE TO SENIOR EXECUTIVE

Moving to a senior executive role brings its own challenges. In addition to leading your own organization, you are likely now part of an executive leadership team. As the leader of your organization, similar to executive responsibilities, you set expectations and the culture of the organization. Your behaviors, actions, and approach to work set the tone for the full organization. Additionally, you need to be thinking of succession planning for the future leadership roles in the organization, including your own, and taking action to develop the next generation of leaders at all levels.

As a member of an executive leadership team, you have a shared responsibility for positioning the entire company for success, not just your business segment. In this role, you also need to find and use your unique voice. Your value is not in being an echo chamber of the viewpoints of others nor being a silent partner. You need to bring your own values, views, and recommendations to the ELT.

Finally, your timeframe for business focus shifts even further beyond the 5-year timeframe as an executive. You need to be considering where and how to position the company for decades of continued success. This shift in focus also means looking externally for changing business, society, and technology changes and then considering how to position the company for a successful outcome.

LEARNING POINT – With the move to a senior executive role, you now have the additional responsibility of helping the entire company position itself for success for decades to come. This means understanding external influences that can impact the company's future and positioning the organization to succeed. Finding your unique voice and actively sharing your own perspective enhances your value as a senior executive. You also need to be actively developing the future leaders at all levels of the organization.

++++++++++++++++

In this chapter, I have outlined some of the key challenges you will face as you transition from one role to another as you climb your Career Tree. I have also highlighted the change in timeframe for business focus as you undertake various leadership roles. As you find yourself moving through these roles, I hope that these points help ease your own transition. One of the best pieces of advice I got from a mentor as I made these transitions for myself was to think about what your boss needs to know and do to be effective at their job. This broadens your perspective and makes you start thinking and acting at the next level of leadership.

REFLECTION QUESTIONS:

- Am I stuck in the actions and responsibilities of my past role? If so, what do I need to do to change my perspective?
- Is my thinking broad enough for my responsibilities? Am I looking down when I should be looking forward?
- What does my boss need to know to make an informed decision? If I don't know, ask them so I can build my own skills.
- Am I doing my own research and analysis to develop my own view and perspective, or am I just echoing the points of others? How am I using my voice as a leader?
- As I get ready to move higher in my Career Tree, who have I trained and developed to do my job? Am I spending time developing the leaders of the future?

SUMMARY OF LEARNING POINTS – ROLE TRANSITIONS

- As a supervisor, your success is dependent on the success of the individual team members. Knowing their strengths and areas for improvement, and building a sense of collective ownership, are foundations for success. Your business timeframe focus shifts from daily/weekly activities to monthly/quarterly/yearly work scope and planning to ensure timely delivery of work product without stressing the team.
- The move to a manager role means growing new skills beyond your core functional skills. You have to become adept at interfacing with other leaders, coordinating with

other teams, aligning multiple teams to deliver results, and working through others to get the results you want. You can no longer rely on just your own personal technical capabilities. You will also play a more active role in setting strategic objectives and annual targets.

- As an executive, your accountability expands beyond just annual goals and targets. You now play a key role in setting the vision for your organization and gaining alignment on direction and deliverables. You need to be looking 3 to 5 years ahead to position your organization for continued success. You have moved into the position where your words and actions set the tone for the group and have a strong influence on performance. Be clear, concise, and encouraging.

- With the move to a senior executive role, you now have the additional responsibility of helping the entire company position itself for success for decades to come. This means understanding external influences that can impact the company's future and positioning the organization to succeed. Finding your unique voice and actively sharing your own perspective enhances your value as a senior executive. You also need to be actively developing the future leaders at all levels of the organization.

Chapter 13

ABCs + (Guidelines to Live By)

Over the years, as I served in various levels and roles of leadership, I created a list of guidelines to live by. I call them David's ABCs +. My hope is that these resonate with you and help you in your own personal journey of leadership, no matter what level you find yourself or how high you rise in an organization.

A = Accountability: Take Accountability for your words and actions. Don't waffle, don't pass the buck, don't blame others. Own up to what you say and what you do.

B = Be Bold, Be Brave, and Be Inquisitive: As you progress through your career, it can be scary to take on new roles, move to new cities, and learn new subjects. To help advance your career, when opportunities arise, Be Bold and Be Brave, seeking the chance to shine. And no matter where you are in your career or what role you find yourself in, Be Inquisitive. Ask questions. Don't assume you know everything. By asking questions, you learn from others, expand your horizons and networks, and let others see the value they bring to the table.

C = Collaboration: As the saying goes, No Man is an Island. The key to broad success (yours, the company, and your colleagues) is Collaboration. Working together brings out the best ideas and ultimately the best results. Build your capability in this area by being open to the viewpoints of others before you share your own. In the words of Stephen R Covey in The 7 Habits of Highly Effective People, practice Habits 5 and 6 – "Seek first to Understand, and then to be understood" and then "Synergize".

D = Delivery: When you make a commitment to someone (including yourself), follow through. Deliver what you promise. Do what you say and be true to your word. Become known for someone who stands behind their word and one who can be counted on to deliver. Your reputation and profile will grow without having to self-promote.

E = Excellence: This area goes hand in hand with Delivery. Whatever you do, do it to the best of your ability. In addition to being known for delivering what you promise, also be known for Excellence in your work and/or product. Again, your reputation and profile will grow exponentially.

F = Fun: Work doesn't have to be mentally and physically draining. Learn to have Fun at work. Many in the workforce will complain about how work is dull, or boring, or a drag. Why? Make friends, celebrate wins (big and small), and be happy. Let your attitude be one of making work enjoyable for yourself and others. The day will go faster, and you will feel better. In the end, you have a say in making work Fun.

G = Grow – Personally and Professionally: As you have read many times in this book, one of my key lessons learned over my career has been to never stop growing or learning. This applies to both the personal and professional sides of your life. Be curious about things, actively seeking opportunities to take on new tasks. Learn new skills. Learn another language (one of my biggest regrets). With this approach, life will be fuller and more exciting.

H = Humility: As the old adage goes, "No man is an island." The easiest way to become one is to be arrogant. A better course of action is Humility. Humility isn't a sign of weakness. Instead, it is a sign of strength and self-confidence in that you don't have to blow your own horn to gain recognition. It is a course of action of doing your best and letting your work and actions speak for themselves.

You may be wondering, "Why stop at H? Why not the whole alphabet?" In truth, I could come up with examples for each letter (okay, Q and X might be a little tough). I wanted a set of guidelines that resonated and was easily remembered. I had originally stopped with F = Fun, but on reflection, I decided that G = Grow and H = Humility were important to include.

I hope you find these short guidelines helpful as you climb your personal CAREER TREE.

Concluding Thoughts

As I conclude this book, let me share some final thoughts about the journey of your CAREER TREE as you Plant the Seed of Your Career, Grow Deep Roots, Build a Strong Trunk, Branch out in Learning New Skills, and Grow in Stature and Bear Fruit.

- Do what you enjoy and be good at what you do
- Own your development
    - Plan what you need to do to be the best you can be
- Hone your communication skills, both verbal and written
- Never forego your personal values and principles
- Build your personal resiliency
- Build and maintain relationships/networks inside and outside your company and industry
    - Colleagues, classmates, other work teams
- Treat everyone with respect
- Never stop learning

I hope that the examples and learning lessons I have shared will help you as you navigate your own CAREER TREE. May you become the best version of yourself that is possible. I wish each of you much success and happiness as you move forward.

Appendix

Summary of Learnings

EARLY YEARS – PLANTING THE SEED

- Don't be complacent. Just because you are GOOD doesn't mean you can't get BETTER. Never stop learning and growing your skills.
- You can always learn something from everyone you encounter. You just have to be willing to accept the lesson.
- You can't grow by staying in your comfort zone. Without pushing your limits, you become self-limiting.
- Success rarely comes overnight. Success is gained by learning from each effort, taking feedback, and incorporating improvement tips. Many times, success is built by many small steps, improving one on the other.
- REPEAT – Don't be complacent. Just because you are GOOD doesn't mean you can't get BETTER. Never stop learning and growing your skills.
- Don't become overly focused on one element. Strive for balance in school, work, family, friends, and faith.
- It doesn't matter if your job is as a professional, tradesman, or in the service sector. Hard work creates value for others.
- Knowing what you don't want/like to do is as important as knowing what you love to do.

- (BELATED) Helping others improve and succeed isn't a sign of weakness. In fact, it is a sign of strength.
- When new opportunities arise, don't be afraid to step out of your comfort zone. Remember, it is a chance to learn and grow. And when you find something you like to do, it's no longer work. It becomes a passion and a joy.
- Life can change suddenly. Pursue the things you love, both in your work and your life.

EARLY CAREER – GROWING YOUR ROOTS AND BUILDING YOUR TRUNK

- When starting something new (job, craft, adventure), put in the extra effort to learn the fundamentals and be the best you can be.
- Don't be afraid to speak up when you feel a request/directive is unethical, immoral, or unsafe or will put you, others, or the company at risk. And if you are the boss, be willing to listen to the input of your staff. Safety should never be compromised for expediency.
- Being good at your craft is the starting point. Working closely with others who are good at their jobs leads to outstanding results. To achieve outstanding results, you must be willing to lean on others for support in unfamiliar areas.
- As you grow your capabilities, be sure to seek out a mentor to help you develop further. They are a great resource for expanding your knowledge, giving advice, broadening your perspective, and becoming a better you, both technically and personally.

- Don't pass up an opportunity to challenge yourself, broaden your skill set, and grow your capabilities. This includes self-study, classes, formal training, or on-the-job training.

- When challenged and feeling overwhelmed, don't feel you have to do things by yourself. Seek out others for advice, guidance, and support. Working together, you can address the challenges at hand.

- While it may not be required for your job, setting and achieving goals for personal development and industry recognition are great motivators.

- REPEAT– Don't pass up an opportunity to challenge yourself, broaden your skill set, and grow your capabilities. You never know when those skills may be needed.

- If given the opportunity to learn from an expert, take full advantage of their experience and expertise. Ask questions, seek feedback, soak up their knowledge.

- As you build your skills and achieve levels of success, be humble. Your success is more than the result of just your personal skills. The support from others very likely plays an important part in your success.

- When faced with differences of opinion (whether technical, financial, operational, or strategic), keep in mind the advice from Covey's *7 Habits of Highly Effective People*: Habit 4 – Think Win-Win and Habit 5 – Seek first to understand, then to be understood.

- When a learning opportunity presents itself, don't let it be a "boondoggle," a trivial or useless activity. Make sure you focus and use the time to build your skills, broaden your perspective, and deepen your capabilities.

MID-CAREER BRANCHES

- As a supervisor, your success is dependent on the success of the individual team members. Knowing their strengths, areas of improvement, and building a sense of collective ownership is a foundation for success.
- REPEAT – Helping others improve and succeed isn't a sign of weakness. In fact, it is a sign of strength.
- REPEAT – When challenged and feeling overwhelmed, don't feel you have to do things by yourself. Seek out others for advice, guidance, and support. Working together, you can address the challenges at hand.
- Stopping a bad project is just as important as advancing a good project. Either way, you need to have a strong technical basis and thorough economic analysis for your recommendations. Let the work speak for itself.
- While building your core skills, two additional skills to work on are communication skills (both written and verbal) and financial knowledge. Being able to clearly and concisely communicate key points and demonstrate the profitability of your work will enhance your overall effectiveness.
- Just because you are the supervisor (or senior member of a team) doesn't mean you have all the answers. Learn to value and leverage the experience of your other team members.
- When facing a tough project (deadlines, challenging deliverables), spend the time to get alignment on expectations and final deliverables. Build on the varied skills and experience of the team members. Don't be afraid to bring different backgrounds together to solve a problem.
- When evaluating a portfolio of projects, remember that a high-level forecast is unlikely to be "accurate" at the

individual component level. That said, there is confidence that the performance of the total portfolio can be reasonably predicted. The key is knowing at what level to trust the information.

- The move to a managerial role means growing new skills beyond your core functional skills. You have to become adept at effectively leading, coordinating, and interfacing with other teams to align and focus your teams on delivering results and working through others to get the results you want. You can no longer rely solely on your personal technical capabilities.

- Helping colleagues succeed doesn't have to be bad for you. As you help others build their skills, they will do the same. Collectively, the enhanced performance across all teams will give greater success than just one segment or team doing well.

- Team culture can't be demanded. Like trust, it has to be built on solid relationships and the belief that everyone is aligned on the shared objectives and will give their all for the team to succeed. Aligned goals and trust drive team success, not individual superstars.

- When you reach an impasse in your analysis, take a step back and make sure "owner's bias" isn't skewing your perspective and clouding your vision. You will be amazed at how taking a different view can change your perspective and your outcome.

SENIOR EXECUTIVE SUPPORT

- When given the chance to broaden your horizons, don't take things for granted. Be curious and put in the effort to truly learn from others. Doing so will broaden your perspective and enhance your overall skills, thereby increasing your value to the organization.

- Often, taking on jobs with increased responsibilities also means increased demands on your time. It is critical to your personal life to find the right balance point between work, family, and friends. Value your time and use it wisely.

- When a project needs your skill set, step up and step in. Take a lead role and don't be shy.

- By building common objectives and agreeing on the process for completing work, you can quickly bring a team into alignment, which significantly helps in overcoming obstacles.

- Working with others who have different views, perspectives, and/or styles can be a challenge, but only if you let it. By leveraging each team member's views and working together, the outcome can be powerful and impactful. Let your differences drive greater value.

EXECUTIVE ROLES

- When stepping into a new leadership role, making a connection with your staff is critical. Being physically present whenever possible significantly accelerates the process of connecting and aligning with your team.

- When called upon to lead others who have recently been your peers, pressing your position of authority is not the most effective means of success. You need to leverage their experience and expertise and seek their input on critical decisions. Showing them respect helps ensure team dynamics are supportive rather than destructive.

- As you start a new leadership role, gaining alignment on critical deliverables for the organization, including focal points for accountability, potential threats, and areas requiring support, is critical in helping ensure early success.

- As you grow in your career, you will be faced with choices of roles to undertake. In addition to career growth, consider the impact on your relationships, especially with your family. While each individual is different, reflect on finding the work-life balance point that is right for you.
- Outstanding performance can create opportunities for growth and expansion but doesn't guarantee a successful outcome. Either way, don't stop your focus on continuous improvement and delivering on commitments.
- REPEAT– Helping others improve and succeed isn't a sign of weakness. In fact, it is a sign of strength.
- When given feedback on performance improvement, don't jump to denial, pushback, or become defensive. Take time to reflect on the key message being delivered and consider multilayered actions you can take to improve.
- When driving change and/or continuous improvement activities, finding champions within the affected groups is critical to jump-start the adoption of the new process and drive the desired results.
- Value can be "created" by outstanding performance. Value is often "realized" by effectively communicating performance levels and identifying areas for further gains.
- While identifying opportunities yields potential value, successfully executing the projects yields value realization.
- When taking on a new assignment, think of it in two parts. First, what skills and experience can you bring to the job that can help you have a foundation for success? Second, use the new aspects of the role as a learning opportunity. This is a vital opportunity to grow your skill set and broaden your perspective.

MOVING LATERALLY

- When evaluating amongst multiple options, sometimes the best questions to ask are not either/or but instead AND. Finding the right balance between choices is often better than focusing on a single option. Also consider alternatives in case the primary options are no longer viable. Developing contingency plans is a great way to build the skills of team members.

- As a leader at any level, you must repeatedly and always communicate clearly the uncompromising importance of safety. You must also be aware of the impact of your words. If you immediately shift from talking about safety to asking about schedule and targets, your comments on safety are undermined.

- When delivering a tough message, expect resistance. Be calm and present your case professionally and purposefully. Engaging with others without becoming overly emotional or loud will give you a better chance at gaining alignment.

- As you grow as a leader, a true measure of your success is the positive impact you have in developing and maturing future leaders. This demonstrates growing in stature and bearing fruit in your late career stage. In many ways, you can receive great joy from seeing an individual grow into an outstanding leader.

- As senior leaders, we need to work hard to ensure that our systems and processes are set up to give equal access to opportunities for every individual to demonstrate their skills and abilities. That is true Diversity, Equity, and Inclusion. The choice of how to respond to the opportunity is up to the individual. With equal access comes equal chance to grow, shine, and progress.

- Always make sure you know the requirements of a task, especially if you are a representative for the company. A lack of understanding/knowledge of the requirements (legal, contractual) can put you and the company in a position of legal peril.

- PERSONAL – One of the most important decisions in your life is the choice of your life partner. Who you surround yourself with shapes how you approach life. For me, I have been blessed to find someone who is caring, loving, supportive, and willing to join me in adventures around the world.

- REPEAT – When taking on a new assignment, think of it in two parts. First, what skills and experience can you bring to the job that can help you have a foundation for success? Second, use the new aspects of the role as a learning opportunity. This is a vital opportunity to expand your skill set and broaden your perspective.

- Even as an executive, broadening your skill set and building on your core skills will position you for roles of greater responsibility and accountability. Be ready to step into those roles.

GOING GLOBAL

- If you find yourself in an area (or country) with different customs, don't just "trust your instincts." Be willing to take guidance from those more knowledgeable.

- Being a senior leader doesn't mean you have to isolate yourself. At the same time, it doesn't mean that you are best friends with all your staff. Finding the balance between leader and friend can be challenging. Learning to segregate the two aspects of your life, and being humble in both, makes each role easier.

- As you take on more senior executive roles, you will find yourself accountable for areas of the business where you don't have expertise. It is critical to leverage the experience and expertise of other leaders on your team. Your job is to put in place the policies, practices, and support systems to help your team succeed.

- A lack of knowledge of national culture can lead to missteps. Be aware and be knowledgeable about cultural norms. You may very well avoid embarrassment from putting your foot in your mouth.

- National culture trumps personal style. Be prepared to change your approach or accept frustration and delays. You may find that the change in approach alters your leadership style for years to come. Your adaptability will also be a role model for other leaders in your organization, helping them navigate their own development.

- REPEAT – Life can change suddenly. Pursue the things you love, both in your work and your life.

- When faced with a new and unfamiliar environment, you can retreat into your shell and close off others, or you can take the (tough) step to put yourself out there, engaging with others, and build new relationships (and even friendships).

- PERSONAL – Never block a sneeze. It's better to wake up everyone in the house (including the dog) than permanently damage your ear and lose your hearing. Trust me.

- When you see problems, you can either point them out and complain, or you can step up to help solve the problem. Be a part of the solution, not a part of the problem.

- As a senior leader, your words and actions matter. You set the standard for acceptable behavior. Set the standard high and live up to it.

- Developing future leaders is a true sign of success for a senior executive. Usually, you lead an organization for only a few years. To position an organization for long-term success, you have to identify and develop the leaders who will follow after you. It is a daunting and challenging task, yet an awesome opportunity.

- Your success as a senior executive isn't measured by how many commands you issue. A true measure of success is how effective you are at getting an organization aligned and at removing obstacles and barriers to let the organization work better. Start engaging with your staff. Ask for feedback. Become the servant leader.

- When your integrity is challenged, you can cave or you can stand tall, even if there are personal impacts.

- REPEAT – Life can change suddenly. Pursue the things you love, both in your work and your life.

- Life and work both come with ups and downs. To position yourself for success throughout the hills and valleys, do your best, keep your word, and serve others.

CHANGING COMPANIES

- Sometimes you have to take a step back to position yourself for future growth. Also, in looking at new opportunities and companies, remember that company culture is a key value for determining your fit in an organization. In some cases, it even trumps compensation.

- When stepping into a leadership role, a key to early success is building connections with your staff, your direct leader, and the other leaders in the organization you will be interfacing with. These connections are the foundation of effective engagement and support.

- REPEAT – Life can change suddenly. Pursue the things you love, both in your work and your life.

- As both an employee and a leader, company culture matters. Building relationships with each other and supporting each other in your time of need speaks volumes. When you feel supported, your commitment and effort are strengthened.

- When dealing with multiple partners/team members, it is critical to make sure everyone feels that their input was heard and considered. Your job as a leader is to create the environment to allow full input and to facilitate the group to reach consensus on the path forward.

- As a leader, you will often interact with others with different backgrounds and/or from different regions of the world. To enhance your leadership capability, you have to have an awareness and consideration of their viewpoints, even if they are different from yours. Considering multiple viewpoints is a strength to be developed.

- As a leader of an organization, when evaluating a proposal or investment, don't let your bias/hope for a successful outcome cloud your judgment of the value of the project. And don't chase the hope for a positive outcome for too long. Sometimes, it takes a failure to teach you how to better evaluate opportunities and prepare for future projects.

- Building and broadening your skill set and experience can and will position you for future opportunities. Making sure others in leadership positions know your capabilities is also important. Don't sell yourself short, but at the same time, don't oversell your background. In the end, let your work speak for itself.

- REPEAT – As a senior leader, your words and actions matter. You set the standard for acceptable behavior. Set the standard high and live up to it.
- Training isn't always easy or fun. But it is important. Never skip your training. You never know when the skills you learn may be called into action. And they may even help save your life.
- As a senior leader, there is tremendous value in understanding your personality/behavior style, learning how to recognize other styles, and knowing how best to interact with other styles. Take time to do an assessment. A couple of my favorites are Merrill and Reid Social Styles and TTI Disc and Driving Forces.
- As a leader, take time to invest in your people. Their personal and professional growth is one measure of your own effectiveness as a leader. It can also be personally fulfilling to see their continued success.
- Misaligned objectives often result in subpar results. As a senior leader, your charge is to encourage teams to work together to reach an agreement on aligned objectives. This alignment is critical to position the organization for success. Get the teams working together, then step back and watch them exceed your expectations.

RETURN TO SENIOR EXECUTIVE AND EXECUTIVE LEADERSHIP TEAM

- In climbing your Career Tree, sometimes you have to go down a few branches to allow you to climb higher in the future. Persistence and focus are crucial to start your climb again. Use the time to expand your network and increase your knowledge of the company.

- A key deliverable for a senior leader is providing clarity and focus on critical success factors for the organization and gaining alignment and commitment for delivering outstanding results. This is not something you can delegate down the line. Own it and make it happen.

- Feedback (both positive and negative) is a gift. As a senior leader, you should be seeking frequent feedback on how you and your teams are doing, especially if you are in a service role. But to make feedback even more valuable, you have to reflect, act, and respond to the input from others.

- As a senior leader, taking time to invest in others to help them navigate their path to success as they climb their Career Tree is a rewarding investment. You likely had someone to help and guide you. Be that leader and guide to someone else.

- Many senior leaders get to that position of stature based on their experience and expertise in a particular functional area, be it engineering, project management, HR, finance, etc. But being an effective member of an executive leadership team demands more. You have to find your unique voice to add to ELT discussions. And don't be afraid to use it.

- REPEAT – When delivering a tough message, expect resistance. Be calm and present your case professionally and purposefully. Engaging with others without becoming overly emotional or loud will give you a better chance at gaining alignment.

- When communicating a tough message to senior leaders, be sure that you have linked with other affected parties so that you are aligned on the problem and also options to address the issue at hand. Lack of alignment and transparency only makes a problem worse.

- As a senior leader, look for those opportunities to help others. But don't approach those interactions with the attitude of "I am right, just do it my way." Instead, to see real change that sticks, approach the interaction through engagement, learning how best to help other groups improve.

- REPEAT – Helping others improve and succeed isn't a sign of weakness. In fact, it is a sign of strength.

- As a senior leader, you will face some tough choices, particularly around personnel assignments, including your own future. In working through the options and recommendations, stay committed to your values and do what is right for the individual and the organization.

- When your role is no longer there, don't check out and lose interest. See it through to the end and exit with grace.

(SEMI) RETIREMENT – STEPPING BACK & SERVING OTHERS BY GIVING BACK

- Retirement doesn't mean checking out and parking on the sidelines of life. Find the activities that bring you joy and reframe your "spare" time to engage in the things that fulfill you.

- As you reach the top of your Career Tree, continue "bearing fruit" by looking for opportunities to use your experience, skills, and expertise to help others. You, too, can find satisfaction and fulfillment as you see others improve.

- Again, as you reach the top of your Career Tree and are looking for the next chance to apply your skills, maintain and grow your network. Keep your eyes, ears, and connections open and active, as you never know where your next and best opportunity will come from.

- As opportunities present themselves, be sure to test them against your drivers and motivators. As you do, you can very well find activities and endeavors that bring your fulfillment even as you reach the top of your Career Tree. Use this time to start helping others in their own career path.

ROLE TRANSITIONS

- As a supervisor, your success is dependent on the success of the individual team members. Knowing their strengths and areas for improvement, and building a sense of collective ownership, are foundations for success. Your business timeframe focus shifts from daily/weekly activities to monthly/quarterly/yearly work scope and planning to ensure timely delivery of work product without stressing the team.
- The move to a manager role means growing new skills beyond your core functional skills. You have to become adept at interfacing with other leaders, coordinating with other teams, aligning multiple teams to deliver results, and working through others to get the results you want. You can no longer rely on just your own personal technical capabilities. You will also play a more active role in setting strategic objectives and annual targets.
- As an executive, your accountability expands beyond just annual goals and targets. You now play a key role in setting the vision for your organization and gaining alignment on direction and deliverables. You need to be looking 3 to 5

years ahead to position your organization for continued success. You have moved into the position where your words and actions set the tone for the group and have a strong influence on performance. Be clear, concise, and encouraging.

- With the move to a senior executive role, you now have the additional responsibility of helping the entire company position itself for success for decades to come. This means understanding external influences that can impact the company's future and positioning the organization to succeed. Finding your unique voice and actively sharing your own perspective enhances your value as a senior executive. You also need to be actively developing the future leaders at all levels of the organization.

Acknowledgments

First is to my wife, Susanne. Thank you for sticking with me through the moves back and forth between New Orleans and Houston and for being willing to spend four years halfway around the world in Brunei. Your creative view of life has made this journey a blast. And thanks to our kids, Rebecca and Timothy, for joining Mom and me on the various moves. Hopefully, we gave you a taste of the world and expanded your horizons.

Thanks to my early mentors at Shell: Jeff Johnson, Chuck Spiece, and Stacey (Pepper) Methvin. Much of my early success can be attributed to the time they spent teaching and coaching a young and brash engineer to be better. Sadly, they have each passed away, and I can't thank them in person. A special thank you goes to my Executive Assistants throughout my leadership roles: Jeannie Kemp in New Orleans, Haslinda Kifli in Brunei, Esther Vallejo in Houston. You had the unenviable job of keeping me on time and on subject. Well done by each of you.

Thanks to the senior executives at BHP who gave me the opportunity of an executive role focused on helping others build their skills and start climbing their own Career Trees.

I am extremely grateful to my editor/publisher and marketing team (Caroline Barnhill and Mark Monistere) at 1 Stage Media. You have been a joy to work with and have helped make this book better.

I would like to thank Dr. Mohammad Heshmati, my co-teacher, for the Petroleum Engineering Capstone course at Mississippi State University. You have become a close friend and helped me with the transition from corporate work to semi-retirement and adjunct professor. I have so much fun working with the students each spring semester.

I also want to thank my Shell colleague, Ernst den Hartigh, for inviting me to be his business partner in the TAB New Orleans organization. Coaching business owners on ways to improve their businesses in ways that change their lives has been delightful. It has given me a chance to give back and help others.

And I must thank my best friend since university, Grant Phillips. You continue to challenge my worldview and keep me humble.

Thanks also to COL(Ret) John M. Horn, Sr., for reconnecting after almost forty years post High School and for validating many of the Life Lessons from his own Career Tree in the U.S. Army.

A big thanks to all my students at Mississippi State University and TAB clients who encouraged me to take my stories and life lessons and make them a book.

Finally, thank you to my GOD for his many blessings, including my salvation through his Son, Jesus Christ.

About the Author

David Purvis grew up in rural Mississippi, the kind of place where hard work was expected and ambition had to find its own footing. He was the self-described "nerd" in a small high school — the kid who loved math and science and quietly dreamed of doing something bigger than his surroundings suggested was possible. A math teacher who refused to let him coast, and a brother whose life was cut tragically short by a drunk driver during David's senior year at university, both shaped the young man who completed his studies at Mississippi State University determined to make something count.

He graduated Summa Cum Laude with a Bachelor of Science in Chemical Engineering and went on to build a 36-year career in the global oil and gas industry — one that took him from offshore platforms in the Gulf of Mexico to boardrooms in Michigan, Houston, and Brunei, and from leading a four-person CO_2 team to managing more than 1,200 staff as Technical Director for a major international operation.

Along the way, David stopped a $500 million project headed for failure, resolved a major underground blowout crisis, helped develop the first Bruneian national to serve as Technical Director in the company's history, and led engineering teams of more than 300 professionals across multiple continents. He also became a graduate of the Shell Executive Leadership Program at INSEAD, earned his Professional Engineer license in Petroleum Engineering, and was recognized throughout his career as someone who combined technical rigor with a genuine gift for developing people.

But David would be the first to tell you that the résumé isn't the point. The point is what he learned — about leadership, about integrity, about the price of standing firm when it would have been easier to fold, and about the profound responsibility that comes with having people look to you for direction. Those lessons, earned through decades of real decisions with real consequences, are what this book is built on.

Today, David serves as a facilitator for The Alternative Board (TAB) in New Orleans, where he leads peer advisory boards for business owners, organizations, and non-profits navigating the challenges of growth, strategy, and leadership. He is also the founder of Purvis Consultants, LLC, where he provides strategic planning, investment reviews, and executive coaching to companies and leadership teams. He serves as an adjunct professor and advisory board member at Mississippi State University's Petroleum Engineering Department and is a Lifetime Member of the Society of Petroleum Engineers. David also serves on the board for several foundations and nonprofits.

He is also a husband, a father, and — as his daughter once reminded him with a Christmas wish for "dads to be home more" — a man still learning how to balance the tree he has spent a lifetime climbing.

Climbing Your Career Tree is his first book.

David lives in New Orleans with his wife Susanne, whose love and support, in his own words, helped him grow in ways he didn't think were possible.